The History *of* Airports

To Roland —

with fondest love, as ever

Chris
xo

Dec '09

Chris Goode
THE HISTORY OF AIRPORTS

Selected texts for performance 1995-2009

ganzfeld

Published by **ganfzeld**
140 Osbaldeston Road, London N16 6NJ, U.K.

First published 2009

Printed and bound in the U.K. by CPI Antony Rowe, Eastbourne

ISBN 978-0-9563706-0-0 (paperback)

for Sam Ladkin

Contents

Introduction and acknowledgements

IT FEELS VERY ODD, as someone who has consistently fulminated against the chronic misidentification of theatre—particularly in British and Anglophile cultures—as a species of literature, to be sending out into the world a collection of texts like this. I have always valued everything that distinguishes theatre as a live art: everything that frames it as a momentarily topical production out of the contingent relations between real bodies and present intelligences; everything that privileges it because it is ephemeral, because it resists commodification, because *you had to be there*. What sits on the shelves of the theatre section of your neighbourhood bookstore, at its pristine remove from the erotic turbulence of the live encounter, is, in its representation of the matter of theatre, as mendacious and loveless and as frankly dead as the rows of butterflies you might see pinned to a card, behind glass, in your local museum.

And yet it seems to make sense to publish a book of this kind, and not only because every so often somebody has been kind enough to ask for one. It makes sense partly because the texts gathered herein are quite various in their forms and appearances. There are cod-scientific papers, there are graphic scores, there are texts that explode over the page, there are love letters and viciously sardonic stand-up routines; but there's not very much here that looks like a play script.

There's quite a bit of poetry, too, and that makes a difference to how I view this collection. For years I have described myself as a theatre maker with a parallel practice in poetry: but the process of compiling these texts has forcefully revealed how exactly wrong the word 'parallel' has been all this time. Not only do the two lines touch, but they overlap, they wrap around each other, they tie themselves in wonderfully complex knots. So my insistence that theatre texts have little validity as independent writings, while poems contrarily have a legitimate life on paper (provided they earn their ink), has quickly come to seem unsustainable. Most of the pieces here are actually hybrids, one way or another: and my hope is that they will enter the reader's imagination not as neatly classified poems or theatre texts but simply as constructs and propositions that will stimulate other thoughts, other actions, of a similarly slippery nature.

We had better be honest and say that "texts for performance" is something of a misnomer. By no means all of these pieces were written *for* performance; it would be truer to say that I have, at one time or another, given public performances of all of them, or directed others in doing so. In fact some of the most interesting and exciting experiences I've had as a performer have been in trying to lift what might seem very intractably page-bound texts—'Fear Feeds Feeling (Phrase Piece)', for example, or the two 'Blurt Studies'—into genuinely live renditions, with all the immediacy and riskiness that that phrase might imply. What makes some of these pieces "texts for performance" is precisely that: the steep challenge that they present to the performer. Perhaps that could be one way of making the book useful, after all. How will *you* perform this stuff?

Because they originated mostly in the context of various theatrical (or musical) projects, almost all of the pieces collected here feel like collaborations. Of some of them, it is exactly literally true: there are texts here which were part-written, to greater or lesser extent, by Gemma Brockis, Harry Gilonis, Jonny Liron, Tom Lyall and Theron U. Schmidt. I have noted more specifically these colleagues' contributions in the 'Notes' section at the end of the book, but I thank them here for allowing themselves to get caught up in it all.

For generously supplying the occasions, platforms and premises that gave rise to these writings, my grateful thanks to: Sue Beresford, Jonathan Bohman, Andrea Brady, Jeff Cain, Alison Croggon, Nate Dorward, Alan Lane, Hugh Metcalfe,

Richard Sanderson, Helen Slater, Keston Sutherland, Martin Sutherland, Lawrence Upton; to everyone at Artsadmin, especially Nikki Tomlinson; to Richard Lee and everyone at the Jerwood Space; to Nesta Jones at Rose Bruford College; to Steve Willey and Alex Davies of Openned; and to Shaun Glanville and the Trustees of Camden People's Theatre.

In addition to those already listed above, many dozens of people were, and are, intricately connected with the making of these pieces and the larger works from which some of them are excerpted, and many more lent support and encouragement: too many people, all together, I'm afraid, to name; though I overlook or undervalue none of them in thanking an exemplary few: Julia Lee Barclay, Joel Chalfen, David Chapman, cris cheek, Roland Clare, Nic Conibere, Dennis Cooper, Lucy Ellinson, Susanna Ferrar, Jeremy Hardingham, Wendy Hubbard, Elizabeth James, Simon Kane, Lynne Kendrick, Sam Ladkin, Sébastien Lawson, Peter Manson, Greg McLaren, Tim Miller, Thomas Moore, Cis O'Boyle, Robin Oakley, Anthony Paraskeva, Neil Pattison, Malcolm Phillips, Tom Raworth, Philip Ridley, Finlay Robertson, David Selwyn, Rajni Shah, Tassos Stevens, Tomas Weber and Jamie Wood.

Chris Goode
London, October 2009

Etienne Montgolfier

[ETIENNE finally frees himself from the sack. He smoothes down his clothes, straightens his hat, and addresses the audience.]

Previous civilisations appear to have invented rudimentary balloons intended to be powered by language alone.

What these primitive people soon found out is that almost all language has roughly the same density as air.

A number of pictorial records akin to hieroglyphs have survived, which all show balloons full of language just hanging in the air in front of the speakers' faces.

Examples of the language used include: 'Watch out!', 'Zoinks!', and 'But we only have fourteen hours to save the earth!'

One can only imagine the torment of these simple early people as they tried in vain to utter words that were less dense than air. What elusive language can they have spoken in their dreams, as they yearned for elevation?

How they must have longed to find the right words that would cause them to be lifted into the air by their own parts of speech, and to live there among the birds and the flying monkeys.

[Escapology, 2004]

An introduction to speed-reading

Aloha Generalissimo! your speed-reading dollars, your plenty, it is to serve you on a platter, thus taking these advice. **How to approach the text:** The text is devil-sticks. The text is "what goes down stairs" i.e. Slinky. The text is one one thousand two one thousand three one thousand monkey on the council lungfish farm. **Tip:** The eyes should move independently. The left eye should overtake the right eye on the straight. The mouth should blow indolent spit globes, the correct embouchure is shown in fig. 8. **Tip:** Hold the text as you would hold a bad red cabbage i.e. away from you and preferably out of the window. Scold it without remorse, say BAD CABBAGE, say that. Stick it in the shredder marked Deutsche Bank. **Tip:** The text is an ornery slut you push a starting pistol up its gaping wimbledon hole it will moan like a blind calf shove it on up. Ways of disabling the text: (1) pin-down (2) half-Nelson (3) "Matt Thorne, the idiot novelist." **Tip:** Make the cat read it. **Getting started:** First read the page as a bitmap. What is a text what a image so on *ad plasmam*. Readers possessed of 'the funk' (see fig. 9) may use multiple algorithms to analyse the stroke edge: oh mother she will go wandering off. I've never had a multiple algorithm. Well then baby take an average. Plunder the good earth. **Reading myths, #1:** "Reading is linear." Au contraire Claire, reading is in a bent hoop belle of oval what blatant Valerie blent is what that, obviously. **How to get more out of the text:** In the first stages of reading, the objective is to obtain as much meaning as possible from the text. Synthetic word-splitting enzymes such as Phonemase can help improve meaning yield by up to 98% per cent / exploded banana republic. Throw me a dry-loving bone here mailman / the pulp wash process: make sure jellification of the text is avoided during concentration. During what. During concentration I think he said. It's more of a blip. If that's a blip I'm Quincy. **Pod:** There is in the town of

Coblenz a poor man who is bewitched in this way. In the presence of his wife he is in the habit of acting after the manner of men with pamphlets, that is to say, of practising reading, as it were, and he continues to do this repeatedly: nor have the cries and urgent appeals of his wife any effect in making him desist. And after he has read two or three pamphlets, he bawls out: "We are going to start all over again". After an incredible number of such pamphlets, the poor man sinks to the floor, utterly exhausted. **Tip:** Hey! Have a shit fit. Do a benny. Do a brassica. Replace every fourth thought with "Bo Diddley" (fig.10). **Tip:** Stick map pins in its outset. Find a sturdy looking-surface. Before it goes swimming down Filibuster Cove change its mind, its arrows, cut its Speedos henry: salt mustard *virgula* shopsoil. Leave it to Beaver at the tan-skin crossroads heading south. **Tip:** Undertake to read the text in a smoky environment. The text will think it is on fire and the words will form orderly queues and proceed to the nearest exit. **Tip:** Disrobe the dirty begging text and lube its wilful vertices. The text is a reverb chasm awaiting steamboat operator's contra-snatch. **Reading myths, #2:** "Reading is a laborious process and is time-consuming." Nothing could be further from the sofa. Get a mandrel bent exhaust system. Install an underdrive serpentine pulley. Grab a witch-hammer. Make your fucking Hispanic pool-cleaner move the book while you keep your eyes absolutely still as if you were in some kind of academic catatonia or waking lifestyle narcosis, pausing once every minute or so to gargle your dark brown spawny piña colada. Allow your mind to wander from (a) sea to (b) shining sea and (c) back again. **Tip:** Phone society. It's society's mess. **Tip:** a note on bookmarks. [insert bookmark note here] **Bullet point:** "When a text, proud of its interior-exterior relations, deceives its reader, then the king should ensure that it be torn apart by dogs in a place much frequented by people." [Holy Book Of The Smurfs 8:371] **How to read this article:** (1) Cut the head off. You might want to hang it upside-down first. (2) Run a little faster than ever before. (3) Make your children pull out the feathers. All except the wings and the anus. Cram the feathers into mother that'll learn her. (4) Burn the skin. (5) Cut off the oil gland. (6) Divide the text into verso and recto. (7) Don't touch the pooping bag unless you are absolutely convinced you are Anish Kapoor. (8) Climb into the refrigerator. I mean live there. I'm absolutely serious. Shut the door the light goes out you're in the dark with the lights out. Jailbait you suck freon issue. What do you want George Herbert Softy Walter etc. For more useful and exciting information about chickens, click here. If your text starts to urinate while you are holding it / Clam rage. Clam cram rage. Bate rage. Premium rate clam-bake chromium rage. More rage types after this message. **Tip:** Check out the periods, the full stops I mean, the full points, they're see they're like little nipples it's such a crying pity they don't make a tongue noise. LA. LA. LA LA LA that's suspense dots. To be continued LA LA LA. Little hard nipples all in a row I'm getting a bit emotional. **Remember:** You have the right to make a citizens' arrest. **How reading is achieved:** The position sensors on the ocular ligaments (fig.11) are used to transmit position coordinates back to the control station, where a graphical representation of the eye is displayed on the operations screen. The logic control processor / pick up turnover / was that a mule or a fog I saw. A disappointing end to a brilliant career. **Tip:** Climb up on a ladder. Have your father climb on the roof. Now both jump at the same time. Who has the most gravitational potential energy? Who do you think will be travelling faster when they hit the ground? **Tip:** At five fifteen in the morning (fig.12) too tired to masturbate watch some semi-recumbent dickweed called Bubble reading a book also called Bubble while a tv camera films him turning the pages (one every eighty-five seconds) and the rest of the housemates are in bed dreaming of a travelogue gameshow they might one day present possibly called Birth Canal or Jackalheads or Foghorn Leghorn's Bunghole Blunder or Dunce-Bothering Almost Live from the Metropole. **Reading myths, #3:** "All parts of a book are of equal value." Quasi-mystical bullshine. Do not read the parts in Latin. Do not read the page numbers. Do not read the bit where she's telling him how she's been hurt before and she can't go through that again. Do not read the pictures. Do not read the source code. Do not read the very very short words (which are rubbish) or the very very long words (which are likely to be medical and therefore indecent). Only read words where the vowels occur in the correct order e.g. 'facetious'. Do not read both L's in the word Corelli. Once you've read the words 'Mormon' or 'gangbang' once, remember them, and you'll never have to read them again. **Reading myths, #4:** "Shab shabi dishab shabi da shahre sham ashub shod. Shishehgar shashido as shashash shisheha shish hesaro sheshsado shast tikke shod." This myth is, actually, true. What **to say in a speed-reading emergency:** I don't see my Audi! I don't see my BMW! I don't see my Buick! etc. etc. Oldsmobile! I don't see my Plymouth! I don't see my Pontiac! etc. my Shrdlu! etc. etc. my Volkswagen! **In conclusion:** Generalissimo, ladies and gentlemen, we are speeding towards our destiny hold the children's soft heads their delicate chins launch the hyper-legible sparrows at the cave-mouth lurch we got a bleeder waits for no man the problem is the paper it's written on it's too hot to handle I mean literally I mean this paper is too hot to Jesus too Jesus too hot to hold—

[2003]

Twenty Minutes in Love

I

Look. Listen. It's simple.

For years your life goes:
clock off, take the lift down to the ground floor,
thank the commissionaire.
Go out into the rain.

It goes: straight ahead and over at the lights,
it goes: chemist's, bookshop, bicycle repair shop,
drunk guy, supermarket, clothes shop, bank,
post office, chemist's, left turn,
shoe shop,
               bus stop.

It goes: wait for the bus.
It goes: all things come to those who wait.

And it just goes like that.
That's how it goes.

And then one day it goes: straight ahead and over at the lights,
it goes chemist's, bookshop, bicycle repair shop,
no drunk guy, supermarket but the wrong supermarket
and the wrong colour,
and the post office looks like it's on fire,
and then it goes: baker's, DIY store,
soaked to the skin, and people staring,
                            and then it goes:
oh well here I am miles from anywhere at dusk again

and then it goes:
this bruise
and how when I look at a light my eyes hurt
and I was soaked to the skin and miles away

                                    and it never quite clears up
look at my arm
can you see the bruise?

And I couldn't remember how to get back home
and I was twenty minutes late.

And it got cold and dark
and the only light for miles around
was far away the post office

                        burning

                                    And I met this
girl, called Anna, and she was twenty, and she had a Mr Bump
plaster where she cut her head shaving. And she told me she
was driving on the motorway at sunrise, one morning in
March, and she'd been driving all night, and the radio had
been playing nothing but her favourite songs all night and
she'd been thinking about a girl she knew who used to look at
her and just look and look and wouldn't look away no matter
what

and then the radio went dead and Anna tuned it and there
wasn't much but static

and then she found a voice on the radio and it said:

I'm coming home
I've been away so long
I've been so cold
Can you meet me?
I really want to see you
Did you think of me?

I thought of you the whole time I was gone
When it was cold
When it was nighttime
In the dark I spelled your name out to myself
A letter at a time
I'm coming back now
I'm coming home
Let me come home

and   Anna looked up
and   she had no idea where she was
and   she was driving very fast
and   she didn't want to stop

because she didn't understand it
but she knew

she knew the sound of her own voice
even on the radio

and she was driving very fast now
very very   fast

        and she had this bruise

II

I should say first of all that I don't even know what this is, what it is that I'm remembering.

I'm sure it was still early but already it was very hot, we'd been all night outside and the sleepiness never really went away anyway, it was like being caned but just on the space of it, the way the space enticed us in so many directions at once. But at the same time, that it was all right just to be still, feeling the sun and feeling that it was enough, that it would all go on, something gentle.

I could barely remember the city any more. Just the people and the city air, the wide streets and the people making their moves. You'd think sometimes they were going to break into song at any moment: and what it's like to move among a thousand people on the brink of song you can't forget. I remembered watching you dance that one time, with the boy who did the caricatures, that embrace that became a slow dance right there. Long before I had the right to be jealous, though I was, but more than that it seemed to cover us all with permission, which was awful, I remember, for as usual I already wanted to kiss practically everyone in the room.

But already moving on, and the warm air and the weird kind of sleepiness, which never went away, it sort of smoothed things out into a radiance. It wasn't lazy, it was spunky in its way, and kind of avid, and it was in that place and that kind of avid time that I especially wanted to kiss you. I loved the look of you, and the promise of it all, like you can love the way that people move at the moment just before they start to move. And that was the place and the feel of it.

Then of course there was a change, a shift of emphasis. Maybe the rain came sooner; something. I'd forgotten rain could be like that, a soft thing, edgeless inside you like a password lost in the memory somewhere. Touching your face for a second and your smile, fleet and strange like a different beautiful person entirely slipping out of reach.

I don't remember a thing about it. I mean I think I've forgotten something so important before I ever really knew it anyway. And impossible to conjure up, like a dream of flightless birds. And I don't know how to move away from it, because it wasn't a place, or even, forgive me, a person. It was like weather, or like time, or like time passing into weather. So I'm staying.

You're taking off your clothes and the window's open and the city traffic and the weather always, here, look at my hand shaking. My car just died, I'm in no condition to drive. I'm staying the night.

III

Pollen count

The carpet in this room is thick with insects,
bottle-coloured and crackling with rumours
like the marrow of mathematics, excavated.
This many insects heated will sublime,
apparently: not liquefy to algebra
but rise into the air again as radio,
air's kernels, its conundrums with pink wings,
invisible to the untrained eye, torrential.

Or: when astronauts have motor accidents,
their little yellow cars are towed away
and lost to us. And then because these astronauts
can't breathe unaided, slowly they disintegrate.
Sometimes their residue will stain a fingertip,
or dry the throat, or settle on a cup.
And then these pixellated astronauts,
like heroes, keep their secrets, and disperse.

So astronauts and insects are the same,
I guess, in that way: drawing the shape of breath
from breath, and making it appear a gift
to hold, still. And in the turbulent
fictions of the air they are our mark,
saying our names back to us while we sleep.
What we let go is how we know we're here,
or how to get back home, or anywhere.

IV

A koan

here is no interior, no skin
behind the eyes:

we fold corner to corner,
touch red to violet, just
skim the colour pool:

vertigo releases light
and a thumbnail maps the station

where one deflected whisper
is the graffito scrawl of
blood clinched in ice;

where *hold tight*
is the name of a metropolis

and love's a star: a thing
to wish upon: sane, steady
and already not where you are

V

Hey Tigerlily,

I've got e-mail now, so at least I can work on the stockpile of things I wanted to tell you.

Firstly, I've changed my route home at night. I cut across Primrose Hill now, and it's made me think this: that the long-distance language of physical presence is light. I mean, people twenty miles away, I only know about them because they convert the chemical energy of their existence into a sort of luminous marker. Each house becomes a *bureau de change* where they trade their individuality for something generic and countable. It sounds like a bad deal but it's either that or subsumption into a dark invisible mass, far away.

The reverse of this process is when we see light and exchange it for presence. Like I think if we couldn't see stars, the idea of aliens wouldn't occur to us. We look up at night and think, ah, someone's home. It might be a million years ago but someone's putting the kettle on.

So I guess if a stranger says to us: 'Got a light?', or 'Spare any change?', either way what they're really asking is, are you there? Are you real? Which is why not answering, if you don't, feels diminishing in a way, and stays like a glitch in your day for a while.

And perhaps it's why the lucent diagrams of chaos drawn by fireworks in a very dark sky involve the heart at such high speed.

Also I want to say that I dreamt of you on Wednesday night. I dreamt a sort of Super-8 movie of you as a kid, you lived in an enormous house and you were playing in the garden, kind of a blur, with your hair in your eyes and your shirt coming off, it was a home movie made by someone who couldn't concentrate, and you as a kid at any moment about to turn a cartwheel or turn into a kite in a high wind. I didn't even chase you but you were beautiful. It helped that it was a silent film so I couldn't say anything stupid.

Did you know, by the way, that the Japanese ideogram for 'thought' is made of two other ideograms in combination: the sign for 'heart' below the sign for 'field'. The heart is the origin of thought in that culture, and the heart makes the thought grow in the field. Did you know that? I thought of you.

I miss you. I miss making love to you late in the morning beneath a skylight of the loft apartment in New York where neither of us has ever been or ever made love but where there is, I promise you, a skylight, and we could be happy. Don't you think?

I'm going to try and send this to you now. I'm not sure what I have to do. I hope it doesn't all just disappear. This is like telling someone your secrets while they're asleep.

I hope you're awake. Reply within seconds or I'll burst.

[20]

VI

outpost

or the punch cost

of the palm's laugh-
line, the smoke-
screen idol, the lust-
food song spoon-
fed to the clock-
work polygraph;

the 'in' in 'in-
joke', when it's just

meant as a joke;

or the aborted screen-
saviour, the rain-
coat at the coast;

the liberty take-
away, the half-
lives we lost

just too soon

to the karaoke.

VII

A charm against disappearance

When we are cold,
light us then, because it is
a temperature held in the dark
of a clenched hand.

When we are falling like water,
then come between us
as a cupped palm, indicating
an end to forgetfulness.

When we are just barely snow,
do not count us then,
and do not let us fall upon heat
and disappearance.

Then when we have become light,
startling through the gaps
of a traditional picket-fence;

and when we are rising like steam,
calling ourselves home
in freewheeling turbulence;

and when we are warm,
no more out on the street,
loco, dealing angry prayers:

we shall swear the interior
of things, noticing

pleasure in odd places:
and we will hold

everything like light
lives inside a closed eye.

Love will settle down

and even our skin

naked wear it:

you

in

I

VIII

(an experiment in withheld laughter)

first locate the rain

isolate it using the standard method
see figure 1

remove the top layer of cloth
& bombard your isolated rain
with the particulars of light

capture the resultant crowd of faces
in a chamber called cartoontime
see figure 2.1

meanwhile stretch your sound band across a gorge
& let the natural force of hopelessness act on it.
results are unpredictable
and may at certain temperatures
become a bit unstable
...so to speak...

no, look, forget it

kiss me up against the back of
figure 2.2
infiltrate my hair with twenty fingers
while employing the techniques for trapping snow
against a dark background
outlined in chapter five

use the accumulated snow
to make Easter

figure 3
expose the bulk of Easter to cartoontime

if you hear me pray
while this experiment is undertaken
you'll observe that only certain parts are audible

these may include such terms as:

gone away

refractive index

glass, shale

skyhook

dormant energies may sometimes be released
see figures 4.1 through 4.4
the likely outcome
might be expressed in standard form
as skin imitating another's skin
returning to skin
in safety

this will result in the flow of charged light
around the wet circuit
and the laughter should eventually be expelled

in case of emergency
flipping channels may depressurize
the situation, at the moment
when we all say in unison:

it's angels versus aliens
let's get ready to rumble

thus if you will be sleeping far away tonight
sleep tight

and should your own dreams crawl
across the pages of this book
then love
      (see figure five)
               do you recall:

because it's simple:

listen

look

[1995-98]

Something & nothing

Smthn.

Smthn.

Smthn.

The stranger's face was slightly the wrong shape.

Smthn.

Smthn.

Who he was, nobody knew yet, but it dawned on them that he'd just come from the dentist's, and you didn't need to be Bananarama to know that he was really saying "Something."

Smthn…,

he said again, drooling down his chin and onto the hot pavement.

Smthn happn.

What is it? said an old man. What happened to you?

This old man had been communicating with dogs, bears, dolphins and insects for years now, and with cats and finches for several months, and with some spinach for about a week, and in fact he was really a very gifted old man in a number of ways.

The stranger could only continue to mumble, Smthn happn, which seemed to be getting them all nowhere fast, until someone realized that the pool of sputum and dribbled blood on the pavement had formed into the shape of a finger, and the finger was pointing at a dentist's surgery eight blocks away. Everybody set out for the dentist's, apart from a little boy called Sandy who had mistaken the finger for an airship and was looking in entirely the wrong direction.

The mob and the police showed up at roughly the same time to find the dentist stuck in the window, half in half out, too fat to make his escape, but too thin to just put a leather coat on and pretend to be a sofa. He was stuck all right, stuck fast, stuck like a stigmatic honey-bee trying to solve a quadratic equation. He sat up there wailing and moaning quite unspecifically about hubris.

[Wail. Moan.]

Observing the dentist stuck half in and half out of the window, one of the attending officers remarked that it "all seemed more liminal than criminal." It was his first ever attempt at a wisecrack in front of his colleagues and he'd fatally forgotten their complete lack of interest in the condition of postmodernity.

Cut to the newsdesk.

—Call this a story? You said you had something for me. This isn't something. This is nothing.

—But the dentist –

—But nothing! Enough with the but everything already. Where's my story?

—But chief, that's what I'm trying to tell you. It turns out the dentist wasn't really a dentist at all. Why no, in fact he was – was – was – was—

Your printer is out of paper.

Please load paper or envelopes into the automatic sheet feed.

[Channel hop.]

You decide.

Is this something or is this nothing?

Is this something [1] or is this nothing [0]?

Is it something

AIRHEAD: Wow that's really something!

or is it nothing?

YODA AS KING LEAR: Nothing will of nothing come. Again speak.

Is it something

SHIRLEY BASSEY: …in the way he moves…

or is it nothing?

POLICE OFFICER: *Come along now ladies and gentlemen, there's nothing to see here, let's move along now please, show's over, it's time for closedown —*

[Sine tone.]

Oh my god she's flatlining!

[Alarm.]

It's a terrible scene, terrible —

I mean really tacky, badly lit, and the make-up looks like economy marzipan —

but there she lies, on the borderline between life and death, and what's she thinking about?

Getting married.

The day she got married for the fourth time, to a man who insisted his name was Scarface, though his chequebook said Paul Edwards. The priest asked if anybody knew of any just impediment why the two of them should not be joined in holy matrimony, and the entire congregation leapt to their feet and pointed at the bridegroom and went *[hand over mouth]* "Oooh! Oooh! Oooh!"

The reception took place here, yeah, that's right, here, right here where we are now —

but it was different back then, it smelled like industrial toilet cleaner, as though everyone was wearing a dab of thinners on each of their pulse points.

She remembers watching in some disquiet as the brother-in-law coughed up a furball in the centrepiece tureen of Pimms, and raising her eyes towards where she liked to imagine heaven, and just as the band began to play 'You Make Me Feel Like A Natural Woman' she noticed that the mirrorball was covered in a thin but unmistakeable layer of hair. Sleek, light brown hair. She'd freaked out and the banqueting manager humbly apologized and climbed up a ladder and gave the mirrorball a side parting. THE END.

Clear.

Shonk. Vzzzzzt.

Nothing.

And again please.
Everybody clear.

Shonk. Vzzzzzt.

Nothing. (Wait, was that a twitch?)

One more time.

Shonk. Vzzzzzt.

And this time she sits up in bed and goes WELL ARE WE GETTING MARRIED OR AREN'T WE?

[In one breath:]

Everybody in intensive care is slowdancing by the marble light of the slowly rotating illuminated toupee, and there's a man dressed in green, standing right by the bed holding two saucepan lids with wires coming out of them and KY all over his gloves, and you can just about hear the sound of the egg sandwiches going a little hard at the edges under the stern halogen lights:

chxchxchxchxchxchxchxchxchxchxchxchxchxchxchxchxchxchx

Is this on now?

That's what my mother used to say.

She couldn't tell the programmes from the trailers.

She never knew whether she had to pay attention yet.

She'd say, Oh. Are we watching this? Are they meerkats, is it gardening, is he really crying or is it a stunt, or are they — are they — are they—

Your printer is out of paper. Please load paper. Your toner is running low. Please replace toner.

The initiands are walking out of the heat haze.

The initiands are walking together out of the heat haze.

They are naked and their bodies are shining.

They are not in an advert and they do not have anything to sell.

Is this on now? Why are we watching this?

I'm just trying to make you feel all right.

[*Trickle through error:*]

I'm just trying to make you feel all right.

I'm just trying to *make* you feel all right.

I'm just trying to make you *feel,* all right?

LAURIE ANDERSON: *So, how do you feel?*

Is this a medicine? Or is it a placebo?

One. Zero.   One. Zero.

The initiands are walking down the aisle of the supermarket.

They are naked and their bodies are shining and their eyes are shining like helicopters at midday and they are wearing flip-flops.

The initiands look at the breakfast cereal but they do not see it or comprehend it.

The initiands look at the fresh fruit and vegetables and they are vaguely reminded of something they had just forgotten a day or two before.

The supermarket tannoy is communicating with the initiands in a language called Cyndi Lauper which they do not understand. They perceive their own flip-flops with a deep ineffable melancholy.

The fruit and vegetables exist in a climate controlled environment. For fifteen seconds every fifteen minutes it rains minutely on the fruit and vegetables. Every tiny regulated cloudburst is preceded by a digitally generated thunderclap. The initiands hear the thunderclap, but they do not associate it with thunder. It very nearly reminds them, but does not actually remind them, of a bad artist's impression of what happens to you after you're dead, drawn by a pessimist with exceptionally poor hand-eye co-ordination on an Etch-a-Sketch—a technology about which the initiands have no knowledge. Just a really bad feeling.

I... I... I... I... I...

Your printer is out of paper. Your printer is out of toner. Your printer is out of patience. Your printer is out of here.

[Channel hop.]

Are we watching this?

[Channel hop.]

It's day 488, and the housemates have eaten Bubble.

[Channel hop.]

Is this on now?

[Channel hop.]

MARK OWEN:

And, final question. If you were to give a child a Polaroid camera and the child took a picture of the sky with the camera and the sky was grey and the child then handed you the Polaroid of the sky while it was still developing but the sky just happened to be the same colour as the Polaroid during the development process, in your opinion, would you say that the picture I've just described is:

   (a) changing
   (b) staying the same
   (c) neither changing nor staying the same, or
   (d) other

Thank you, and the same question with regards to your memory of this event after one calendar month. In your memory would the picture be:

   (a) changing
   (b) staying the same
   (c) neither changing nor staying the same, or
   (d) other

For the fourth time in as many days, Ralph Macchio was experiencing a complex of ethical, not to say metaphysical, conundra, as he licked his own spunk off the face of Noriyuki 'Pat' Morita.

These sequels to *The Karate Kid* seemed to be becoming more and more frank in their depiction of alternate lifestyles.

When Mr Morita, who had taken over as screenwriter, director and producer of the last forty or so in the series, had initially suggested to Ralph that to show a deepening affection between the characters of Mr Miyagi and Daniel would be to strike a blow for all those who still believed in the American Way, Ralph hadn't fully appreciated the frequency and clarity with which such a blow would be presented.

As it was, Ralph was proud of some of this work. The content may have been explicit but there was no doubting its integrity. And after all, wasn't it he who had told Pat often during the making of *Karate Kid 3* that he wished to steer his career in a more adult direction.

It was just a pity that, without mass audiences, it had been necessary to cut back on staffing and facilities in recent movies. Indeed, ever since *Karate Kid 18*, all of the films had been shot in Pat's garage, with Pat's brother operating the single borrowed camcorder, as well as working as assistant director, make up artist, key grip, best boy, mouse wrangler and principal unit fluffer.

But in fact, as Ralph sucked the dregs of his coagulating spooge out of Mr Morita's bonsai beardlet, he became aware that he couldn't see the brother, or actually anyone with a camera, anywhere. It felt like it was just the two of them. And nobody said Cut.

All through lunch, nobody said Cut. Ralph picked at his California rolls forlornly. He couldn't figure out why the shot was going on so long, why no one was saying Cut.

They walked on the beach after lunch. No one said Cut.

They watched Jeopardy and Futurama. No one said Cut.

They arrived at the point in the script where for various plot reasons Daniel has to smear wasabi on his butthole and sit down on a devilstick, and still no one said Cut.

Finally, as they got into bed that night, Ralph hissed to Pat, Are we still rolling? At which Pat gave Mr Miyagi's trademark inscrutable smile, which was all the answer Ralph needed. Tired and a little saddle-sore, he sank into an impeccably cinegenic sleep, with Mr Miyagi's voice ten thousand miles away like the sea whispering: Wax on. Wax off. Wax on. Wax off. Wax on. Wax off. Wax on. Wax off...

Your printer has left the building. Your printer is sick of your excuses. Your printer despises you. Your printer deserves better.

This man was a writer, or considered himself a writer; but he earned his living teaching English at a prep school in the sticks.

One night, marking his pupils' essays, he was dismayed to hear a radio report about a frenzied knife attack conducted by a madman in a Japanese school. He found the cliché personally offensive. Why were all knife attacks described as 'frenzied'? Were there no other varieties? Was a whole chapter of human potential being disqualified by the laziness of journalists? As he paused to refill his Parker Concord with red Quink, he resolved to make an issue of this tiresome and infelicitous banalité.

Next morning, with Form 3F arrayed before him like a clutch of little yellow caterpillar eggs, he strolled into their midst and embarked on a lugubrious knife attack. He sauntered up one aisle and mooched down the next, stabbing a witless infant here or there as the mood took him.

Pausing for a while to stare idly out the window at a gardening incident, he turned back and dispatched a further dozen or so goggling tweenies, spearing them languidly as though they had been coldcuts at an August picnic.

And so he pottered unsensationally about, slicing those wee mites at whom he could just about be arsed to lunge, until the bell went and it was time, ironically, for handicraft.

Only then did it start to ferment in his mind: What would happen now? If anything?

Cut back to the newsdesk:

—Lugubrious?

—Apparently, sir.

—That's no fucking good.

—No sir.

—What else?

—Um... well, a local man fell over in some milk.

—And?

—And... we've got a picture of him pointing at the milk.

—Beezer! We'll run with it. Get a quote from Glenda Jackson.

Your printer got all pissed up on shandy. Your printer is sitting on the top of Primrose Hill in all the fucking rain. Your printer is disconsolate. Your printer still loves you but it cannot live with you any more. Your printer is drunk and horny and wishes it were dead. Your printer is printing out a seemingly endless text of its own devising. This is how it begins:

ngngngngngngngngngngngngngngngngngngngngngn

The dentist spits two teeth onto the floor. He's never been hit so hard in his life. He looks up into the obscure face of the good cop and into the illuminated face of the bad cop. He's exhausted. He doesn't know what else to say. Let's go back to the beginning, says the good cop.

How many times? says the dentist.

How many times?

Her name *was* Lola.

She *was* a showgirl.

The initiands have finally found what they were looking for. In the middle of a ghost town, on a morning hot as dust and dry as old moths, they have found him. His name is Sandy and he is still looking up at the sky, waiting for an airship that may never come.

Is this changing or is it staying the same?

Is this in motion or is it still?

Ralph Macchio stands like a crane on a piece of silicon the size of a pinhead, looking out at the morning surf, and his nipples are still smarting and he's missing his mom and dad, and he sings to himself:

> You make me feel
> You make me feel
> > *Are you faking this?*
> You make me feel like a natural woman

BBC ANNOUNCER: But let's listen again to that song at half speed

> *[half speed, tremolando]* You make me feel

What you can't hear is the subliminal message that's running backwards through this song. Here our engineers have isolated that message using an ordinary trowel. This is what Ralph Macchio's really telling you. Can you hear it?

> Is this sound – or is it silence?

> Is this sound – or is it silence?

> Is this sound – or is it silence?

> Is this sound – or is it—

[2001]

Riddle

My first is in CRASH but not in BANG
My second's in HOLD and also in HANG
My third is in MARK but it isn't in BRUISE
My fourth is in SLIP and also in LOSE
My fifth is in REMISSION
My sixth and my seventh are in LOVE
My eighth sits in the BUS STATION at one a.m. when the
      blood comes
My ninth bit my twelfth in SPITE
My tenth and my eleventh fought like cats and dogs until the
      cows came home
My twelfth forgave my ninth
My thirteenth lost to sleeping sickness how I miss him
My fourteenth smiling says it's another lovely day tomorrow
      we can go sailing
My fifteenth oh my beloved fifteenth fall asleep all over me
      again

My whole is in SHOCK let us be quiet it's over there's nothing
      to see

[The School of Velocity, 1997]

Icarus Day

There's a village on the island of Icaria which my father visited when he was my age. Every year they hold a festival, whose climax is a kind of public contest. A dozen young men every year are chosen to compete, the youngest maybe fourteen, the oldest twenty-three. They spend all year in preparation for this one big day. They're making wings. They're going to fly. They find their feathers, their wood and thread and wax, and take eleven months to build the finest pair of wings they can.

When competition day arrives, the boys queue on a promontory, looking out to sea, in their underwear and wings. An official gives a signal, and one by one they leap into the air.

If the wind is kind, and their wingspan is sufficiently extreme, it's maybe fifteen seconds till they're drowned. Their parents watch the whole thing, choked with pride. Tears are frowned upon, though my father said that every father that he saw that day, his hair was white.

Weeping and bewildered, my father asked an old man why they did it, why they sacrificed these boys each year. The old man closed his eyes and smiled and he replied: One year, my friend. One year there'll be a boy who lasts a minute.

And then?, my father said.

And then, the old man said, and then the next year…

The sky was very blue.

Do you have a son?, my father asked the man. Or did you?

The old man smiled one last time. Like a stone, he said. Just like a stone.

[Puckerlips, 1997]

Six Postcards

for Jeff Cain

Jean-Michel Basquiat, 1982

Fit to his vacant lap the painter's radiant cat
scowls oblivion. It is as nothing to a pet,
>> how some high varieties of discontent
>> never even reach their adumbrated winter.
Thus, the slow perpetual fall of the gracile Basquiat.

Hanging Paws, Waikiki, 1932

What is the proper compass of the pioneer?
Grey in recession, black in the in-fight of his hair.
>> They look on a man tending to a mannequin.
>> But what in the picture is changed, if anything,
if none of the creatures shown has even been lonelier?

Bilbo and Max, 1995

Loveliest of flowers, perhaps, the chameleon's iris;
or that brave-faced explorer whom the komodo outstares.
>> All facts, like all children, are similar:
>> their hot alien bodies make them familiar;
how they stay up all night redrafting our obituaries.

Doberman, 1990

Words like butter fry on a doberman's hellbent tongue;
a brilliant dissident lantern philosophically spun.
      Matter: the trees are full of psychopaths,
        birds bang rocks, and seeds subdue the grass.
Nothing lasts longer than a song that's sung in anger.

Rene Magritte and his dog, Brussels, 1944

Night and my re-occurring dream, open as wounds;
the air here pricks the conscience of my inert hands.
      My touch is even, but my wife is actressy.
      Here looms the charcoal greatcoat of bureaucracy
and my dog has no nose. I wonder: how I wonder.

[2002]

Apparition of the crowd enclosing Mario Merz

No

less

than now,

drawn near as

mist to Eriskay,

figured out on fingerless gloves:

the garden tally, low breves of twisted fibreglass.

Dead centre: shows up to stare out one possible seed bell; step, pink noise, colourless soap,

step: next to fixity, division, temazepam *volte-face*, the implacable currency of shit, some old neo-neo seeks a frame

with gilt in good nick. Next step: shuck your chrysalidic sleep-garb. Pop out, honey, park and ride, barnstorm the haywain: end of brand. Remark: a strip is something you wear. Whip up the eye-whites till they stiffen into peaks; chuck raw meat at non-dogs,

no birds in the birdbath. We drowse beneath gelatine sheets. Count time down, breathe out breathable lace, an ecstasy of politesse, le jazz hot, *mea culpa*, date-stamped ectoplasm. Your dinner's in the formicary. Later that same night, a furore dribbles neon down the Mall, Peter Mandelson coughs ten grams of spunk into a napkin. Step out: stretch a leg, a point, a limo, now they are paying us in coffee, paraffin, tallulah, now there are boys born without shoulders, how will they ever learn ping-pong? One filthy old *grandpère,* ogling the shut-up seaside, pissing on lemongrass. That dread cadre, fronting up to biff an old dead stuffed giraffe, makes Sunday's shallows somehow dangerous. Gunfire, pencil-point, the mishandled sherpa, this is a picture of us in the elevator, going up. And here we are, coming down, spreadsheet, graffito. Now they're paying us in whiskey, skiffle, raffle tickets, coke. The men all acquiesce. All men do blow.

Saw this, adamantine not before: wassail time, not yet that capriol, a hazchem festival, break it out, stick it. Stick your digital mote, penury in corpuscle flats. This sound stride, cast out the pips from seasonal, specks from *courante,* oblivious liposuction, no split floe, no unspecific light. Dead dried pollwiggle, some apparent meteor stroke match-head, used for punctuating blanks, shear off, devolve in cataclysm. Is this a statement? Only so: charcoal, yes, or sulphur, now coming up sunflower yellow, bubbling under, liquefied state metronomes, *un souffle au coeur,* link membranes, link black septum, link a lack of evidential bruising spite. Touch of strange synchronic phosphorescence, maybe. Those eventual flights of angels singing *sol-fa, sol-fa,* cab for Carlo Giuliani, matter, splint: the panic buds: the ice press below. Here. Where. Hear. Hoar. Ha-ha. Hue. I struggle to breathe. Art halo: shark-attack. I dream on the diagonal.

Behind Station Analogue (original version)

not yet—
or not yet suitable; or
yet drooling by way of apology,
dismissing the wall. and
on, still to unwrap.
J's tryst with Eleanor takes place here,
behind station analogue,
next to the sirius pudding fete,
over to the left.
addicted to the lonelier kind of flightpath
monkeys, she traces the perimeter
with a shuffle. soon a state
of emergency, or advance this,
arms in knots to move it along
a bit. bring gameboy, bring
seahorse, to get seahorse pierced.
lift up the hair. kiss
the unreliable imprint there.
put head on timebomb glow setting,
make the port link alert, go Italy,
go history, go fact and atoms.
go to sleep on a chain.
signals through pocket semaphore,
a hard cock to suck according to
the rota, not yet made out,
the fuzz strike where the city
is most like a bird and where the
bird is most like an oven, there,
fold out from the pelvic
floor to the available body zodiac.
in demo mode, the place of
speed and difficulty
in the new origami, go lip-

balm, go sift, go totally skin-
back, all in the cycle of fall,
spin. the city shoots ink
onto her tits and face.
the last circus steamtrain has now
departed, even the dogs
fuck off. hate more
instead the ghosts that ruin
the body curfew,
thus finally like hands, up
into the push-up snow.
I have wronged them,
both, by precipitating a
severe health crisis. they
remove the top layer of
cloth, test it for presence of
honey. it is like that time,
yeah, the foetus in clay-space,
the blonded ramifications
of the aerial continuity error.
the mud-spattered easels, that
thing they did that they called
needing something. or it was just
a ghost, or a place to hide logs in.
glasshouse J insinuates himself
(thinking of it)
into the conch ornament,
it's like celebrating christmas
at easter, with the blossom out.
oh he says I can't do it.
with her across his body he drowns
his fingers, all but walks out, makes
anemone convulsions.
his bloodcount sort-of recovery
gets made posh in the flicks,
of course, and the autopilot
is sent home in disgrace.

Eleanor says, this is the end
of the road for us, J-boy; heaven
says, if you honour us, we do not
understand you; and then it's
almost time for the last cartoon.

[2000]

Chris Burn

at the outset this stitCh in scape time: holding

still, the skate paper sHoreline coming up on your left

another hollow faiRground, lit in wheel-shapes, pink & tin.

somebody calls for a paper engIneer so that more of the world should pop-

up, they would put a most fuckable dead sentry on fire Stakeout duty

against which Backdrop we are holding

hands; the exact might of someone instantaneoUs

ballooning with liteRate dare, catching on to scare tactics,

stooping to touch their spatial gaNglia, their gang-leaders in exile.

in the city it might seem the caChe garland is in a state

of lethean mismanagement, the sHredder churning late into the night,

but the secretary's earpiece confirms outRight that you compile spirit & weld

a disordered polonaise as an Introduction to the fire escape.

a keeper of the secret shade of senSory aphasia,

nocturnal, insatiaBle, bearing down, agreeing to raise
the stake, the narrow paper cUt, that short slit in the hypothalamus, &
a single bacterium in your palm, you eventually floweR and sit upright,
but now struggling to sustain, now the Neck brace buckles, now nothing.

you are oblivious to the power cut; your downpour jaCking grace,
reclaiming the steel juice out of sHeet torque
it is the stave set down in the umbrage of a dRumstick claw or periodic washer
& so delicately scoot up, shearIng from recourse to and not to neutrino
whereby the zero-mass & one item or lesS mutes the flexor voice in an instant
of sheer saBle pitted against braille.

possibly when your tea comes in a paper cUp you are
more inclined to relax, moRe able to let go. then one night you sit
for ages head on oNe side, a kid thinking about god.

in tandem we were tacitly Chasing the event lizard
one time, and you said to step aside for a grassHopper robe,
but we are muddled up in scaRlatina and beginning to sweat.
on the other side we could watch the clock and the sentImental onion yielding
pre-speech tokens, a puffin Stranded on ice, a metal elbow shapeshifter,

a black diadem in a corporal frame of Beeswax and paraffin. or in hackney
the cello says hello, the flUte says for god's sake let me go, & wherever
you are you know to be the yes-maker, authoR of air shapes,
not their guardian, nor the diligeNt bird-man, not even; and so

by rubbing, choking, you, Chris, chuck out vivace flecks in a curving jet,
& the ordinary minim tone-wHelps tick in the popular grass. how so
steadfastly this man pinpoints the ideal Rhizome, its veterinary codes!
lastly tonight you are Indexing the downstream supercharger,
slaking, fusing, lopping the cutthroat Shock of the especial shape of tact.
you are taking dictation at a typewriter full of rubBer bullets.
in perpetual reconstrUction, the principal stone and jab,
still patching the microgroove, still might get heRe soon, thanks
to the teak, the shale, their stabilised iNtent, you suddenly grab a skyhook.

Three wishes

When we meet again, the next time,

what do you suppose the weather will be like?

When all this shit's died down,

when this crazy war is over...

sometime before sunset...

Out in the field.

That's where you'll find the battle hero.

But for now, let's all go back home to our cats

and our barking frogs.

Everything's upside down here, man, everything's so fucked.

Can't see my hand in front of my face.

[his horses, 2003]

lady m.

to be of no sex
but here

to feel the cruelty in nature
how the land lies

to protect the wound
from healing

to write letters by no light
and sleep till noon

skip / to do it
searing just do it tick

to jump the life to come
to rush the stage

to get naked and to never
never give it back

to dare to fail
screw your courage

to settle for less
than terror

to falsify
a known love

to be here now
and soon again

[his horses, 2003]

Present moment

My present moment has me by the throat.

    a paper field to cut through

                Then stand with us:
    The West yet glimmers with some streaks of day.

    a hand's turn
    the ghost of a chance

    you stand it
for as long as it is beautiful.

                Hark, I hear horses.

    count to four   three four
           His horses go about.

    a night air
    the hope of a kiss

             A light, a light.

I'm sorry. Look up. Look, look up!

         It will be rain tonight.
           Let it come down.

    a night swim into difficulty

Fly good Fleance. Fly, fly, fly.
See Fleance fly. Fly Fleance fly.

[a burst of unintelligible noise]

I can fly.

    a grey area, still;

            the son is fled

and   the brother is fled; and
the father and
his generals and his phantoms and
the brother and the son are fled and everything.

[his horses, 2003]

rilke

his heart
his stronger existence
his falling
his latest rebirth
his solitariness
his godhead
his trident of terrors
his chest
his innermost insight
his mother
his brow
his presence
his lips
his heart
his way into your secret heart
his littleness
his spaces of night
his fate
his restless future
his sleepy eyelids
his inward world
his inner wilderness
his heart
his own roots
his little birth
his forefathers
his young veins
his heart's curtain
his house
his massive hide
his widowed skin
his hands
his ascent

his risk
his onrushing world
his darkened sound
his mother
his imperious choice
his reclining figure
his luck
his sight
his footsteps
his silent fate

[his horses, 2003]

A Dictionary of Quotations

Everything that's said in a whisper is completely true; it cannot be otherwise.
George Bernard Shaw   1856-1950

Oh my true and individual love. Don't you see that your companionship and your body are no more separate than time and death?
Robert Browning   1812-1889

Even with your hands around my throat I am still marvelling at the muscles in your arms and shoulders and the line of your lip. What an incredibly stupid situation. I'm such an asshole and so are you.
W.S. Gilbert   1836-1911

I find the constant rain here easier to bear if I imagine it to be the consequence of an electrical fault.
Friedrich von Schiller   1759-1805

Let's get high and watch the sun come up. We'll go home and cook eggs. I want to fuck you in the shower and hold you tight while you come. I think you're awesome. Truly.
Blaise Pascal   1623-1662

That it should rip out the heart of every other conversation. That the clothes you stand up in should be made of the most fragile paper.
John Milton   1608-1674

Radio is a kind of tattooed sleep.
Petronius   **died AD 65**

Gratitude and recrimination are two hands each drawing the other.
Henry Ford   **1863-1947**

The phenomenon of instantly wanting it again, lest it should become too apparent what it really is.
William Hazlitt   **1778-1830**

There is a photograph of you tucked inside every book I own. I guess I can't help losing my place.
Sir Walter Ralegh   **1552-1618**

It is no accident of evolution that we do not have the capacity to forget at will, or to close our ears while driving.
Friedrich Nietzsche   **1844-1900**

For years I lived under the delusion that the words 'hopeless kiss' were a perfect anagram of the word 'keepsake'.
Simone de Beauvoir   **1908-1986**

Loving you in this way is like a poor man winning the lottery and burning all the money.
Nikolai Gogol   **1809-1852**

I am trying to remember something my friend Anna said to me.
Noel Coward   **1899-1973**

It is no braver to stop crying than it is to start.
St Augustine   **354-430**

How can I call myself a motherfucking writer when I can't find
a language to reach the complexity of your spit drying against
my skin?
William Shakespeare   **1564-1616**

The reason I can't forgive myself for everything that's
happened is that it was all your fault.
Henry Wadsworth Longfellow   **1807-1882**

Let's just find a place to have lunch. I'm sick of arguing.
Oscar Wilde   **1854-1900**

The kite dream is not available in the shops. The airstrip
dream is not available in the shops. The band-aid dream. The
orchestra.
Pablo Picasso   **1881-1973**

I'm only sitting here because I don't want to go to work and I
don't want to go back home.
T.E. Lawrence   **1888-1935**

Shut up. Fuck you. I am trying to describe something
profound. The least you can do is listen.
Lao-Tsu   **604-531 BC**

Participation is civilised. Mere endurance is barbaric.
Lenny Bruce   **1925-1966**

Dear Dad, this town can be so lonely. My room is cold and it's only mid-autumn. I wish you would send me something. I don't know what.
Friedrich Hölderlin   **1770-1843**

If you don't want to be a part of my life, get the fuck out of my life.
Martin Luther King   **1929-1968**

How you came to be by my side at this precise moment, that's a good song. Sing it again. Please. Sing it for me. I'm begging you, please.
John Donne   **1572-1631**

Nothing is closer than fear or more distant than the object of fear.
Martina Navratilova   **born 1956**

It strikes me that there are fewer ways to recall you than there are to lose you.
Jean Cocteau   **1889-1963**

Growing into adulthood is the transition from believing that the stars are impossible to believing that they are simply very very unlikely.
Joseph Stalin   **1879-1953**

There are three ineffable things that you keep in your house: secrecy, nakedness and spiders.
Marie Curie   **1867-1934**

Exclusion is always a punishment, no matter how benign the authority.

George Crabbe   **1754-1832**

Are you travelling alone today? Did you pack your bags yourself?

Ezra Pound   **1885-1972**

It saddens me to think that you can't be involved in a car-crash while swimming.

Voltaire   **1694-1778**

I feel totally betrayed by the circus. I wanted to run away and join the circus but it's rubbish and all the animals are sad.

Aldous Huxley   **1894-1963**

We are walking barefoot across a field. This of course is a lie or some kind of mind game.

Marianne Moore   **1887-1972**

Do you remember our first date? We stole an ambulance and drove it around at high speed. We went through red light after red light, and you said, baby, it's going to be like this for ever.

Anton Chekhov   **1860-1904**

If pain is as incommunicable as you think then there's no hope for this conversation.

H.L. Mencken   **1880-1956**

[his horses, 2003]

Lives of the Great Composers

ALBENIZ	/* makes no sound */
ALBINONI	/* if full moon, may howl */
ARNOLD	/* mews or hisses */
AURIC	/* roars */
BACH, CPE	/* growls */
BACH, JC	/* squeaks, as a rodent */
BACH, JS	/* squawks, as a bird */
BALAKIREV	/* hisses */
BARBER	/* buzzes (killer bee) */
BARTOK	/* grunts (or speaks own language) */
BAX	/* neighs, as an equine */
BEETHOVEN	/* wails, as a tortured soul */
BELLINI	/* gurgles, as liquid or through saliva */
BERG	/* burbles (jabberwock) */
BERLIOZ	/* up to here are animal noises */
BERNSTEIN	/* wakes up others */
BIZET	/* rattles bones (skeleton) */
BLISS	/* grins, smiles, giggles, and laughs */
BLOCH	/* says something or other */
BLOW	/* imitates others (leocrotta) */
BOCCHERINI	/* intelligent brute */
BORODIN	/* generic traveling companion */
BOULANGER	/* "Stop in the name of the law!" (Kops) */
BOULEZ	/* army and watchmen expressions */
BRAHMS	/* "Please drop that gold and follow me." */
BRITTEN	/* "Thank you for freeing me!" */
BRUCH	/* "Take off your shirt, please." */
BRUCKNER	/* "Hello, sailor." (Nymphs) */

BUSONI	/* vampiric seduction, Vlad's exclamations */
BUXTEHUDE	/* asks for money, or berates you */
BYRD	/* berates (demons) or intimidates (Wiz) */
CAGE	/* astral level special monsters */
CAVALLI	/* your class leader */
CHERUBINI	/* your nemesis */
CHOPIN	/* your leader's guards */
COPLAND	/* demands payment, complains about shoplifters */
CORELLI	/* does a consultation */
COUPERIN	/* asks for contribution; does cleansing */
CUI	/* resists fire */
DEBUSSY	/* resists cold */
DELIBES	/* resists sleep */
DELIUS	/* resists disintegration */
DONIZETTI	/* resists electricity */
DOWLAND	/* resists poison */
DUFAY	/* resists acid */
DUKAS	/* resists petrification */
DUNSTABLE	/* see invisible */
DVORAK	/* levitation */
ELGAR	/* water walking */
DE FALLA	/* magical breathing */
FARNABY	/* displaced */
FAURE	/* gauntlets of power */
FRANCK	/* clumsy */
FRESCOBALDI	/* can fly or float */
GABRIELI	/* can traverse water */
GERSHWIN	/* can flow under doors */
GESUALDO	/* can phase thru rock */
GIBBONS	/* can cling to ceiling */
GLAZUNOV	/* can tunnel thru rock */

GLINKA	/* needs pick to tunnel */
GLUCK	/* hides under objects */
GOEHR	/* mimics, blends in with ceiling */
GOUNOD	/* can survive underwater */
GRIEG	/* doesn't need to breathe */
HANDEL	/* no eyes to gaze into or blind */
HAYDN	/* no hands to handle things */
HENZE	/* no arms/legs to kick/wear on */
HINDEMITH	/* no head to behead */
HOLST	/* has no mind—golem, zombie, mold */
HONEGGER	/* has humanoid head/arms/torso */
HUMMEL	/* has animal body */
IBERT	/* has serpent body */
IRELAND	/* has no solid or liquid body */
IVES	/* has thick hide or scales */
JANACEK	/* can lay eggs */
KHATCHATURIAN	/* regenerates hit points */
KODALY	/* can see invisible creatures */
KRENEK	/* can teleport */
KREUTZER	/* controls where it teleports to */
LEONCAVALLO	/* acidic to eat */
LISZT	/* poisonous to eat */
LULLY	/* eats corpses */
MAHLER	/* eats fruits */
MASCAGNI	/* eats both */
MASSENET	/* eats metal */
MENDELSSOHN	/* players mayn't poly into one */
MESSIAEN	/* is walking dead */
MEYERBEER	/* is a lycanthrope */
MILHAUD	/* is an elf */
MONTEVERDI	/* is a dwarf */
MOZART	/* is a giant */
MUSSORGSKY	/* is an orc */

NIELSEN	/* is a human */
OFFENBACH	/* is a demon */
PACHELBEL	/* is a guard or soldier */
PAGANINI	/* is a lord to its kind */
PALESTRINA	/* is an overlord to its kind */
PARRY	/* is a minion of a deity */
POULENC	/* always male */
PROKOVIEV	/* always female */
PUCCINI	/* neither male nor female */
PURCELL	/* monster name is a proper name */
RACHMANINOV	/* always starts hostile */
RAMEAU	/* always starts peaceful */
RAVEL	/* can be tamed by feeding */
REGER	/* wanders randomly */
RIMSKY KORSAKOV	/* follows you to other levels */
ROSSINI	/* extra-nasty monster (more xp) */
SAINT SAENS	/* strong (or big) monster */
SATIE	/* throws boulders */
SCARLATTI, A	/* likes gold */
SCARLATTI, D	/* likes gems */
SCHOENBERG	/* picks up weapons and food */
SCHUBERT	/* picks up magic items */
SCHUMANN	/* would like to steal the amulet */
SCHUTZ	/* wants the bell */
SCRIABIN	/* wants the book */
SHOSTAKOVICH	/* wants the candelabrum */
SIBELIUS	/* wants the quest artifact */
SMETANA	/* wants any major artifact */
SPOHR	/* waits to see you or get attacked */
STANFORD	/* lets you close unless attacked */
STOCKHAUSEN	/* wants something */
STRAUSS JR, J	/* waiting... */
STRAUSS, R	/* < 2' */

```
STRAVINSKY      /* 2-4' */
SWEELINCK       /* 4-7' */
TALLIS          /* human-sized */
TAVENER         /* 7-12' */
TCHAIKOVSKY     /* 12-25' */
TELEMANN        /* off the scale */
TIPPETT         /* generated only once */
VARESE          /* not generated in "hell" */
VAUGHAN WILLIAMS /* generated only in "hell" */
VERDI           /* generated only specially */
VICTORIA        /* appears in small groups normally */
VILLA-LOBOS     /* appears in large groups normally */
VIVALDI         /* can be genocided */
WAGNER          /* no corpse left ever */
WALTON          /* creation frequency mask */
WEBER           /* has been encountered */
WEBERN
WEILL           /* has been genocided */
WOLF            /* has been extinguished as population
                control */
XENAKIS         /* player recognizes egg of this monster
                type */
```

[2005]

Backstage Rider for Baby P.

The artist requires tranquility.

The artist requires one brackets one eight-foot table covered with a white tablecloth.

The artist requires one brackets one comfortable white non-folding chair.

The artist requires one brackets one telephone, white, ex-directory, unknown number. One brackets one telephone stand. One brackets one telephone directory, white throughout, all names and numbers removed.

The artist data source has failed to initialize. Testing: 255 255 255.

The artist requires one brackets one TV with VCR stroke DVD and cable hook-up. Please ensure that the following channels can be received: the Discovery Channel, the Disney Channel, Extreme Sports Network, the rolling news.

The artist requires one brackets one massage table in a separate room, with cordon, white, so that access to the table is prohibited without exception, including the artist and his representatives. White earbud-style earphones. White noise.

Come in sentinel. Testing: 255 255 255.

Foal in distress diagnosed with Overo lethal white syndrome; euthanized.

The artist requires one brackets one beaker of milk. Not semi-skimmed, not from powder, not UHT longlife, not soya, not rice, not Jersey, not sourced from endangered creatures, not from cactus, not even milk, not now, just the promise of milk, or the promise of nearness to milk at some future occasion.

The artist requires one brackets one handful of drinking straws. White or transparent or imaginary.

Supposing (now) that 'white horse' was nothing other than 'horse'.

The artist requires one brackets one piece of fruit, white or off-white.

The artist requires one brackets one bowl of plain M&M's. Decolourised. One brackets one box microwave popcorn, no butter no sugar no salt. White berries. Albumen omelette. Flavourless sugarfree gum.

The artist requires two brackets two 20 oz. bottles of Gatorade correction fluid and one brackets one small bucket of ice.

The artist requires one brackets one clutch of soft-boiled quail eggs. Flour. Styrofoam. Salt and peppermint fondant. Foam and exemplary dove. Please come in sentinel. Come in come in. Pearl sentinel. Cloud cap sentinel.

The artist will require a plain white aura. Chalkdust. Copydex. Chyle and myelin.

Testing: 255 255 255. Input/output operation failed. Store failed. Update failed.

Of things that are white, only some are polar bears.

The artist requires one brackets one platter of snow on snow.

The artist requires two brackets two cube shaped boxes of white aloe Kleenex tissues. No fewer than four brackets four white towels. Twelve brackets twelve large dark towels at 3pm.

The artist requires one brackets one large assortment of fresh cut Casablanca lilies or gardenias. White or colourless or implied.

Cephalanthera austiniae, or phantom orchid, which produces no energy for itself.

Twelve milk teeth. A little bit of coconut. Infinite veils. Albino seed. The toolkit does not recognize the function being used.

The artist is not accustomed to wearing his laminated pass backstage. Please brief security accordingly and ensure that the artist's identity is generally known.

NZE-28838 No identity descriptor.
NZE-28839 No persona descriptor.
NZE-28869 Certificate expired.

The promoter will supply overnight security coverage while the artist sleeps.

First Aid may have a presence near the stage area but not actually in the stage area itself during the artist's performance. A basic first aid kit may be required. Cotton wool, porcelain, A4 premium inkjet paper. Lab mouse. Obliterated sentinel. No distinguished name provided.

No professional cameras. No professional video recorders. No professional audio recording devices. Small non-professional cameras are permitted.

NZE-28757 Attempted to allocate 0 bytes of memory.

NZE-28758 Memory release failed.
NZE-28822 No seed.

The artist will require some quiet time during the day.

The promoter will supply two brackets two wireless radios. These may be abandoned or destroyed. Ivory sentinel.

Swan on swan. Please respond.

NZE-29249 An unrecognized state was passed to a cryptographic function.

The artist will not require water.

[2008]

Lapse

pan cross rooftop stamens
all abruptly first morn
and bleach out in altercate rake   in pencil stub
and threaten jacked-in road
works   chalk and boron lob collision
telltale axle weep entailed   and blanking nets
to cream out basic number suicide

cough starts breath   trapped
in bottled error   and longed-4 uh scape
and compressed animals lucking out on data churn
packed dark beneath these
show-home rearguard tenant stocks
and warning rise in lime and solvent paper-
freaks spun out on polar viewfind

shunt keening wets and fanbelt paranoia   sluts
on twock alarm   and blanket rated chemistry
plus minus or one   like a compound lapse
in fake dusk   boredom chamber lot speaks
salary reverse   and leave the choker running
beached on latchkey reef   in
ogre welts and paranoid   got painterly

in spray-on logic   son you're no son
house   skunk buttermilk caress   in checkout grade-
tests   tab   tab tab bit slide belongs to coma princess
in a leap   and roll   and parascend
too late now to stoop to understand
the roar of the crow   it is as similar
across itself as ice-cream

in-patient clam at its width in battery truck pig
out on solpadeine   pent error float
in carmine ache said ache in dub-plate
tetanus doubt   wreak veal scam   stole
everything   stole you   stole
you stole everything you stole   and
the fault was always yours   skied   lofted

turn around and run

[2003]

The steel workers' proposal for the decommissioning of Beaubourg

Start into sleep sleep the truism 'frigidaire'
the emu 'today' kiss kiss poor plastinated Scotus:
      which gosub homesick tight to the gut projection
      fail fails to convince. Mr Bojangles eats dog,
      tap shoes. Aghast at 'The Dead Sea Experience',
      the number of the beast you dialed has not been
work works like a dream go to work on an edge go
pet a hairy flipchart are you receiving

over. Shame is her swimsuit-round manifesto, lime
mint soap up the wretched ball queen perfidious
      sow / up for gonzo dog treat paddle-assed
      hokum still still selling in Japan see adipose
      four. That wrecking-ball trustafarian
      guinevere trapped in the afternoon concrete
prairie flip flip six second glimpse of Duran Duran,
or the chemical wad that blinds the part-time

poodle valet. Gin and alfalfa mousse it's for washing the
car with, or maybe Heimlich Manoeuvre's the
      name of a German porn director.
      Are we asleep yet? How does the honeycomb
      get in the hive? Now yellow round the tree
      and trumpets shall sound (novelty goddamn
door chime funniest thing) your sheet of interests
and accumulations and multiplex whatnot kitty kitty

tube sox my but the LAPD are so
vulgar. What do you point to? Evidence
      swig say vanilla essence burn up the hissy-fit
      carpool lane like grease and slash or

lightning. Hands turn spin thrift uptake
inhibition every one wants to be
childlike. Script says 'cheep cheep', mother says
never wear diamonds to the ob-gyn we say

stow it. We saw Fanny By Gaslight it's a
band you freakazoid. Nothing ventured nothing
earwax everyone stay stay calm the
millipede in the salsa what's he doing the
backstroke slash-fic butterball spell spell
license as in driver's license
as in rammed to the hilt on cranberry meth
stroke scrotal bouillabaisse up your chimney howdy

pardners. Free's free. Free as the tawny doodad.
Free as a kite in the reckoning up of critical
influence using avoirdupois for the
craic dude huffing a dream from the bag the
milk came in and we have twenty-one
dogs and they're all called Arson damn we
stand in the park 'n' shout Arson Arson
twilight verdigris thriftstore parakeet underscore

Jim Beam doobie doo Whitney's an oreo
whore. Dionne's wig's on funny honey look at the
sky ha made you look. Let's kick it.
Teenage girls always slit their wrists in the bath
week in week out you can set your
watch and Jesus comes like a gift in the
cereal. He's a healthcare magnate. Sure you do. Sure
you do. Sure. It's a matter of private conscience.

Knife. Knife. What in the picture says knife. Where
you live that goes knife. Kissing his boyfriend's eyelids
knife. Pride in authority / grace in deferral
knife. The climate deranged in Kyoto
matinee knife. Knife by the way of

leaves that fall and the boyfriend sleeping
barely near as adrenalin when the emergency comes.
How they will face their long-lost families, dearly.

[2004]

Rare motorcade, arterial bleed

for Mathieu Burnel

Peaches yeah OK or cauliflower this harmless
burden is irrelevant, how will we face a necessary
black and propane history in the crux of a devious
court? The midnight news replaced by linocuts
and narrative tapestry? What way we fly, swim,
croak at the last and sudden, turning wool; man relax
in a demolished house in oviform lamplight batons
hit undo   redo   undo   has one-step memory like a
hummingbird strung out on PS2 and chocolate treacle
windshield steering column marshmallow artefact,
scart to the night sky, route through scuba swallow
and the glad hands down. You kids rope me in.

This is a foal stampede. Their lachrymose klaxon
drizzles down the entry-phone like absent dad spat
butterscotch, his vendomatic pop-shot jenny
droning twilit on like the last fat chop on the slab.
The journalist says popcorn into his daughter's lap.
Let's play strip monopoly. Let's play stripsearch
brutal up till first light terminal four. Let's play strip
wire. Strip data protection. Strip John Paul. One
finger one thumb keep moving. Every two cents
boyhood hero pleads sing anger down the speaking
tube, the redundant horses dream of Uhu. What's
the sex disease you contract alone in your room?

Optional console carry-case. This is nearly enough
to explain the hot malevolent documentary:
American lipids and gash oil drain the colour
from a televised history of spats or flip to how
the Partridge Family starved to death in an unlocked
room full of meat and cereals. Meanwhile the relaunched

culture channel has a counter-tenor fired from a
cannon dealing patriot coloratura, singing blood price
and the sundance clot and Indiana Jones was a
landscape gardener in a flippy-floppy cerise hat.
Rebound. Cling, peaches. Cryptosporidium beat loud-
hailer beat nothing gets harder faster than teen cock.

Daybreak. FX chorus. Cheltenham ladies' gingivitis. Weak
as a kitten. Here's an oral tradition diagram in a
PowerPoint presentation to do with skin dogma.
Cut to the quick chase: dial up the boychick eyeline
cam. We are (circular breathing) speeding up the
body gameplay, swift slam crash the admin cortex
checkbox cervical vertebrae scapula thoracic
vertebrae tailfin cockpit travelator runaround
bracelet cherry Vans red channel, fallback, pants.
Swallow. Swift. Lumbar vertebrae. Rear view mirror.
Dog in the garden, basking idiot smile. Language
is the scab that falls away when the rift's healed.

Give way to night terrors. Hark the timeshare merman
going down on GI Joe in specialty MSG aphasia.
Concentration is the element itself, kiss in a blaze
insert stock salmon footage twitching jerking which
is the death throe which the shape you make in
retro-vogue swoop ego vortex monument ideally
do you really? Lean upstream in the face of Steven
Spielberg's semen spate and what is you is OK here
and I can feel your ribs it's OK even through your
t-shirt. And the distance. And the unexpected first inversion
chord and beach reject and reject spoon and repair
split counter the dust wound counter pupils confront dark.

Slender comrades. It are plural. We were always falling
over   ourselves   and this   in that it finally ends
here, ungiving grip on a jacknifed vesicle   undo
redo   vesicle undo   redo vesicle the blooded wad

pumps on the way that scrap metal breeds bees
in horror film blame fatigue in death dab blague overkill.
Not king of the road not not the great pretender when I
vomit it is not an antic decline cherryade not mere
val-de-ree not yay-high spirits not fuck childlike figured
through lamb decline bleat toxins, washable ink, not
tone-deaf loco parentis just not one two three four not
just totally fucking not follow the bouncy ball.

It's self respect: three four: you stop on a dime.

[2003]

Gay twist varial disaster revert

(12.iv.2004)

                              how in love's
                  late place you drive down the
                       strip your convertible
            language   the slipstream by night
        and the fountain lit-up panoply   shifting down
        and the breeze grace touch to the city   ask you
              how is your body local to me? how
          now   the kindness you cling to   fast too
            fascinatingly fast   the air gone turmoil
                  glitch in the nervous system
        the heart application hangs   and the lights go
        prince to pauper to prince to pauper to prince

        my tremble script   not held by the hand of the
                  skin adept   all birds and animals
                novices made of glass   in view of your
              turning away   ask how do you keep your
              promises?   where do they measure a kiss in
                  teslas? the firmament in banjos? Secret
                  Squirrel in a polytetrafluoroethylene
                  body-bag?   this is the deal hand here
              the proximity flare and the fell chaparral
              of your never-so-broken voice   until
        the vandalised man at the Icecapades sings out
              once   and for all   your sweetness

        your innovative need   reworking a space craft
              mark my / how we love these sounds for
        the words they make   each tongue in the other
              mouth   itself a commitment to public
        speaking   ask in your dialect how to pronounce
        the eventual body undress   or the hurtling upwards
              wall   and the rewritten skyline   based on

what   on the love breaks down what you say into
birdseed   where's the emergency entrance?
how do you dive off the ground?
for body read frame   for inscribe read
persistent desire read modernity   frame you say prove it

home to go   left there   longer   a spineless
thing   but you make daybreak the south pole
everywhere I face is north   then this is the
X-43A scramjet   where we are
seven times the speed of sound oh scramjet
birdie to you   my life in code   ask
how many years   the rest   and the firework
sky and the national skatepark   it's all
done with electromagnets   just
for you   you're curving back   you right here
travelling at hand   my love set out in the field
you arrive before you leave   at mach this

[2004]

Campfire Variation #4

SCOTT: Getting away from everything feels good.
MIKE: Yeah
SCOTT:

                                            whatever,

              Yeah.

MIKE: Yeah   . Well, you know,   like, like

              yeah.   I don't feel
              . I mean, I feel like   , I feel like   , you
         know   .

         I don't know.
         Pause.
                                      I mean
                                                          you
         know, I don't know, I don't feel like   ... I
         don't feel like   I mean
              , you know,   I
         mean, you know...

SCOTT: I... ███████ I mean...
MIKE: I don't know. Whatever.

███████████████
                    I mean ███████
SCOTT: you mean █████████████████

MIKE: I know, man, I know, I know. ███████████
              ██████████████████████████   you
know, ███████████████████████
████████████████████
              ███████ okay. ████████████

Pause.

████████████████████████████
        Yeah. I know. █████████████
████████████████
        Yeah. Well, I don't know, I mean... I mean, ████
              ████████████ you know, █████
████████████████████████
              ████████ man. ...Well, ████████
man. ████████████ You know ████. I
████████.

SCOTT: All right. Come here Mike. Just sleep. Come on.
             Just go to sleep. Come on.

[Past the Line, Between the Land, 2003]

The History of Airports

I BEGAN, APTLY ENOUGH, in Chicago, home of O'Hare, the busiest visible airport on Earth. I was there as the guest of Dr Jack Lincoln, who had been a student of Eugene Aserinsky when, as part of their research into electroencephalography in the sleep laboratories at the University of Chicago in 1953, Dr Aserinsky and his colleague Nathaniel Kleitman discovered rapid eye movement. REM. The ophthalmic murmur of the dreaming mind.

Now, their former pupil had something new to add.

Magnetic resonance spectroscopy, an imaging technique beyond the dreams of Aserinsky and Kleitman, had enabled Dr Lincoln to identify and decode the division of the dreaming brain into its specialised areas, or sectors. There are four sectors, Lincoln told me, of approximately equal size. The first is the area of the brain that is most active during dreams of what Lincoln calls 'the terrible and the mundane'. The second sector is associated with dreams of sex, public nudity, and buildings on fire. The third is concerned with home, with recognising it and knowing how to get there; and the fourth — one quarter of the whole cerebral territory of dreaming — is taken up with flight.

I was with Lincoln one night when he demonstrated to me the phenomenon now known as Lincoln's Gambit. Using electrodes to administer a mild stimulus simultaneously in the second, third and fourth dream sectors in the brain of a sleeping fifteen year old male, he was able to induce REM in the subject. The boy was then abruptly awoken, and Lincoln asked him: Where are we, right now? Instantly, the boy replied: Don't worry. It's OK. We're at the airport.

This response has been replicated across almost every individual in a sample of some three hundred subjects, including many, Lincoln avers, who have never been inside an airport, or are autistic, or sightless, or who have lost relatives in civil aviation disasters.

The really interesting question, though, is this. Would the same results be achieved if we were testing Lincoln's Gambit in the nineteenth century? Or the ninth? Or further back even than that? Has the idea of airports lived inside us for as long as we've dreamed of sex and home, and of flight?

It is hard to say. In the evolution of the airport we perceive, as with rapid eye movement, merely a small and cumulating betrayal in the material world of the activity of the human imagination. There was no *first* airport, no statement of intent. We could bookmark the first paved runway, developed during the Great War; or the rudimentary Newark airport of 1928. Or we could look backwards, to the Rose Window at Notre Dame, to Tallis's forty part motet, to the Sermon on the Mount. Or forward to the major edifices of the virtual sublime, or the nodal termini of remote viewing expressways.

In fact, we might as well begin in Altamira, in northern Spain, 25,000 years before the Common Error. Here, on the walls of the famous caves, stone-age man used fat and dyes from the bodies of destroyed birds, and the colours of the scorched earth, to capture for the first time his vision for the TransWorld terminal at John F. Kennedy airport in New York: a vision which would take nearly eight hundred generations to be realised.

Only a few millennia later, again in Spain and southwest France, the same cavedwellers made sculptures of rudimentary airports out of soil, moistened with saliva and baked in the sun. These models, with their dense interior networks of chambers and galleries linked by numerous passageways, would on completion often be inhabited by termites. In some equatorial regions even today, termite nests, or termitaries, of almost identical structure can often be seen.

It's thought that these termitaries may also at some time have acted as amplifying chambers for the aural traces of complex communications between termites, who, it is argued, must have used their own dreams of flight as a platform for decoding the intentions of the human architects of the prototypical structures. We are familiar with dancing bees, but have tended to overlook the subtle and evasive storytelling techniques of these termites.

Here, at the end of the twentieth century, some philologists are reaffirming the previously discredited theory of an etymological link between the termite and the terminal. Their Latin roots appear separate – 'terminal' deriving from *terminus*, a boundary or end-point, and 'termite' from *terere*, to rub. Many scholars now suspect, however, an earlier commonality of origin: a single word combining the two notions, and meaning: the desire to chafe against a limit. Or: the will to break through.

Did the termites of the paleolithic era succeed in making such a breakthrough? We simply don't know. But we will always be tantalised by the celebrated fossil (number 300.157 in the London Natural History Museum) which appears to show termites in rows of seats, with their backs to each other. If you haven't seen it, imagine a child's drawing of a microprocessor.

Clearly, then, the *idea* of the airport predates not only the reality of air travel but, in some respects, the idea of the aeroplane itself. And this delicate conception, of the airport as a tenet of prelapsarian harmony and universal intercourse, obtains even while we perceive the airport *as it is lived*: as crisis and crucible, as a ulcer in the undifferentiated sheen of decadent globalism.

How, then, shall we move towards a clearer understanding of the relation between the material airport at the end of the millennium, on the one hand; and on the other, the unarticulated *sense* of the airport that has been endlessly detonated with the human heart for the last thirty thousand years?

Again, this is a voyage of enquiry which could be boarding at any one of a multitude of gates, and which could lead us in several different directions, and indeed dimensions. The in-flight movie could have men wrestling with bears, or tiny figure-skating old women, or a computer-generated twister whipping up a whole model village in a vortex of revolting air.

But let us begin with the case of Thanksgiving Island.

This small, fiercely nationalistic state had long considered itself deserving of a fine airport, but was unable to reconcile this with its principle of economic and cultural isolationism and total self-sufficiency in all things. Until, that is, some bright spark suggested that not one but two airports should be built on the island, thus removing the otherwise necessary implication of the reprehensible desire for foreign travel.

As it turned out, because of the small size and mountainous topography of the island, the two airports had to be built right next to each other, with their runways overlapping at points. This proved, however, to be incidental, as no aeroplane ever came within three miles of either airport at any time during their operational life. Not that this represented any impediment to the social alchemy for which all airports are responsible.

On the day of the grand opening, the departures terminal, to the east of the island, was, by all accounts, buzzing: attendant onlookers and enthusiasts mingled with those individual entrepreneurs who saw in the airports an opportunity for personal gain. Before long, these tradespersons, entertainers and petty criminals had constituted a microcosmic black economy, and the severe concrete shell of the building became host to a proliferation of exotically coloured parasite booths and residencies. The authorities turned a blind eye to this eruption of roisterous iniquity, keen as they were to make a success of an airport without any other kind of traffic.

Meanwhile, the west terminal, built to accommodate the arrivals there would never be, was downplayed from the start. It was staffed and grudgingly lit but there was little interest or circulation. Most visitors quickly became embarrassed and returned to the east.

However, as the weeks went by and more and more of the population of Thanksgiving Island streamed into the east terminal, with its complex of shanty houses, fairgrounds and hot chicken stalls, a few individuals began to arrive in the west. Always alone, these were the outcast, the damaged, the infirm and the chronically lost. And there, in solitude, they waited.

By the eleventh week, it was apparent that everybody was living in the airports.

In the twelfth week, the multitude who had gathered in the departures terminal simply and suddenly departed. Which is to say that they vanished, leaving only their possessions, their tents and their photographs, their dogs and their photographs of their dogs. No one ever knew how or why.

The ones left in the arrivals terminal, apparently, remain there to this day, in solitude, continuing to wait.

Are there lessons here for the future? It's hard to think about perspective when, as we know, in a single airport minute, whole hand-to-hand wars may be won and lost, and we have often seen a hundred thousand microformal presidents of the United States of America rollerblade into an oblivion of collapsed Muzak. All the ventilation filters leak a cold yellow mucus, the travelators warp and turn turtle. The ineffable congress of lovers—

AS TRAILED IN PERPETUITY BY A QUARTER OF THE DREAMING MIND

—is reclothed and neutralised into tantric safety demonstrations and the bleak irradiated opportunity to watch blockbuster movies mapped down to the size and scope of an animated scab growing on the back of a wounded headrest.

To many observers, this all suggests that the airport will only be able to support the near-exponential increase in the people's demand for homecoming if it evolves not as buildings do; but as do animals, towards an immaterial system of uninterrupted thought.

As a first step, advances in the technologies of sub-atomic tensility may mean that, within thirty years, permanently unstable airports based on mycoproteins, synthesised *in vitro*, will be capable of handling 128nine billion passengers every second. Meanwhile, researchers at Stanford University continue to pursue the dream of the *airlinac*, or passenger accelerator, wherein travelators of several hundred kilometres in length would be able to accelerate passengers to an energy of 30-40 giga electron volts.

As the materiality of the airport retreats, we'll also see the phenomenon of misplaced congregation on the up and up. Already we are used to seeing four thousand people standing in a field with their luggage around their ankles, thinking they are going somewhere. Researchers into the extra-sensory, meanwhile, worry that partial airports may spontaneously appear as the result of some cultural trauma, and remain trapped in a non-space with all the departure information scoreboards blinking eight, eight, eight.

In some ways, this is not unlike the ancient Sumerian shadow airport in its concentration on *implied*, rather than actual, air travel. The shadow airport pre-set a number of goals that, for engineers still grappling with the concrete airport, remain the defining grails of their science: for example, it was completely resistant to wind and water erosion; it needed no lubrication; it looked great on film; and, above all, during the night hours it took up no space at all, making it ideal for today's impacted urban areas. For many, it remains puzzling that we can put men on the moon, build space stations, you know, a whole bunch of that ant-eye-gravity kind of shit; and yet material airport scientists sit up night after night in their Victorian outhouses, trying to hammer rudimentary shadow airports out of lightweight aluminium and magnesium alloys, and covering them in black feathers, while even now the wolf's at the fucking door, these impy-seals.

No wonder the air traffic controllers are nervous wrecks, little fuckers, pouring out of their bedrooms and into the hallway, bleating about jam, about how they can only work for a few seconds at a time before their antennae are on the fucking blink and all of their nerves and organs have to be replaced. See them! Look at them! Pitiful grubs! It's easy to forget that we are all responsible. That it is every citizen's duty to control air traffic when we see a violation being made. These feeble runts are sort of stillborn heroes. We should celebrate them once a year by crying a lot and going back to bed.

Maybe in time we'll become used to the reality of airports weighing as little as 1.5 pounds and standing only ten inches tall, airports which will to all intents and purposes die at the age of around eleven years, unless some screwy hovercraft magnate drowns them in a sack. Maybe in 2020 we will be used to there being 1.4 billion cubic kilometres of airports on the earth, enough to cover the whole United States of America with airports to a depth of 99 miles, rolling on, surprising us in the morning, coming like Jehosaphat out of a clear blue sky.

Surely, then, women and men will always dance in airports, here and from a height of several hundred kilometres, dancing, just dancing, all the doo-dah day, dancing right up to the limit, and holding our breath and wanting to survive for longer still, and dancing through the limit and into the sky on the back of some ancient stone.

[The Consolations, 1999]

President Lincoln's address to the waiting room

[The tiny PRESIDENT LINCOLN mounts one of the waiting room chairs and starts to speak to the others in Greek. MARIE CURIE simultaneously translates into English, while HELEN KELLER improvises a sign-language version. After attending to the President's speech for a little while, the MONTGOLFIER BROTHERS and HARRY HOUDINI begin to play a musical accompaniment and eventually essay a remedial dance routine, a bit like The Shadows.]

My fallow Americans:

It is surely a measure of the esteem in which I was held as your sixteenth President that during my term of office I was only shot twice.

The first time, the bullet merely penetrated my hat.

The second time, I was at Ford's theatre—a theatre very like this one, with fine rococo features and magnificent plunging architraves—to see a play called *Our American Cousin*. In truth it wasn't a very good play and I had spent much of the first act contemplating the number of Maltesers I could insert beneath my foreskin. When my interest in these speculations passed, it occurred to me that I would find the evening tremendously enlightened if a gunman were to burst in to the State Box.

In actual fact I could not have been more wrong. For when, rather ironically, a gunman did burst in to the State Box and twat me in the back of the noggin, I found the experience left me not so much enlivened as dead.

As is the case with Presidential assassinations, the Vice President was installed in my stead, and indeed he did tolerably well in the post until he too was assassinated while on a lamping trip with friends who mistook him for a moose. In a top hat.

His successor, the erstwhile Speaker of the House, also acquitted himself decently for slightly less than a week before being shot during a hysterical fracas at a national spelling bee. He was replaced by the President *pro tempore* of the Senate, who lasted just thirty-six hours before ending his own life in what appeared to be an autoerotic assassination error.

The Secretary of State was installed and assassinated.

The Secretary of the Treasury was installed and assassinated.

The Secretary of Defense was installed and assassinated.

The Attorney General was installed and assassinated by six separate assassins, who, to their great credit, had formed an orderly queue.

The Secretary of the Interior was shot up the anus by a dinner lady.

The Secretary of Agriculture was pitchforked to death, and then his dead body was assassinated.

The Secretary of Commerce had his throat slit and gold-tipped bullets inserted into the wound.

The Secretary of Labor was assassinated before his installation as President was complete. The Secretary of Health and Human Services was assassinated as he stepped out of his limousine on the way to his own inauguration. The Secretary of Housing and Urban Development was assassinated while he read the telegram which confirmed his appointment.

The Secretaries of Transportation, Energy and Education were all assassinated while they argued heatedly about the line of presidential succession. The corpse of the Secretary of Education was then used to beat to death the Secretary of Veterans' Affairs.

The Secretary of Homeland Security arrived for his Presidential inauguration to resounding cries of "Dead man walking!" However, against all odds, he survived in the post for the remainder of that term, and for a full second term, and became one of the most popular and revered political figures of his generation. ...I'm kidding, of course. They took that sucker out like the trash.

At this point, the line of succession having been exhausted, a variety of Presidents were tried out, from senior White House staff including the Chief of Staff and the Director of Communications, through to an array of PA's, pen-pushers, perverts and sub-postmasters. All were summarily assassinated.

By this point, with the average term of a newly installed President down to just 19.8 seconds, it was becoming harder to find volunteers to do their patriotic duty. A special act of Congress was therefore passed to allow for Presidents to be drafted. It was at about this time that America had her first black President. And her second. And hundreds more. Proud times indeed for the Civil Rights movement.

The accelerating incidence of Presidential assassination seemed to be unstoppable: until an amendment to the Constitution made it possible for the first time for all age restrictions on the office of the Presidency to be lifted. Then, following a televised pageant watched by millions, little Janet Ben Romsey was elected as America's first schoolgirl President. In her fuchsia-coloured taffeta party dress, Janet captured the nation's hearts during her inauguration as she sang the immortal words of Whitney Houston: "I believe the children are our future. Teach them well and let them lead the way. Show them all the beauty they possess inside." Finally, it seemed, the country had a President everyone could love. Unfortunately, Janet's disquisition on 'the greatest love of all' came to an abrupt end when she was assassinated simultaneously by over eight hundred masked gunmen, and all the beauty she had previously possessed inside was suddenly visible across a wide area of the back wall.

And so it continued until 2001, in which year nearly four thousand people, many of them children as young as apples, were assassinated for no better reason than they were the President of the United States of America. Something had to be done—and it was done. A further amendment to the Constitution made provision for other species to assume the mantle of Commander-in-Chief.

Since then, it is estimated that anything up to 35 million chickens have served as President of the United States, at an average rate of one every 2.7 seconds. Almost without exception they have been assassinated. A lucky few have died of natural causes while in office, or fallen downstairs. One was liberated by animal rights activists, and went back to its job as a filing clerk at the U.S. Patent Office. One became a carny. One had a hit single on the urban charts. One was briefly married to Liza Minnelli, but relented, and returned to the White House, where it was fucking assassinated.

In November 2004 the rate of chicken Presidents of the United States is steadily increasing by approximately 1.1 chicken Presidents per second per second. By extrapolation it is likely that in 2005 the rate of chicken President acceleration will itself increase by anything up to 1.85 chicken Presidents per second per second per second.

In 2005 America will have enough chicken Presidents to fill Ford's Theatre two thousand five hundred times.

Two thousand five hundred and fifty, if you rip the beaks off.

[Escapology, 2004]

Bush Unit

BUSH UNIT, properly George W— Bush, primitive technology for the fractional distillation of air.

Regions of the sky exhibiting two or more of the formal or chromatic characteristics of spaciousness are rapidly condensed and passed through the rudimentary alveolar canals of George W— Bush. In this unit, the air is cooled further, until it approaches stasis. It can then be separated into its six broad constituents; which are: prayer, hydrogen, nostalgia, the dry soil, platelets, and tar. A cursory examination of the uses and properties of each may help us to appreciate the contemporary importance of the Bush Unit.

Prayer is most commonly used in advanced industrial societies as an anti-ozone agent. Despite its complex molecular structure, prayer is considerably less dense than Standard International air, and may be applied for example to Caucasian women's hair, which is then said to be 'flyaway', orienting itself (as it will) theotropically, i.e. toward the god region of the noosphere. The property of flyawayness is taken to connote fertility, heterosexual prowess and full-term pregnancy: any lapse from which prestige model in the consumer may therefore be effectively countered by prayer.

Hydrogen and nostalgia, between them, have been the principal fuels of the American imaginary for almost seventy years. Being less volatile than hydrogen, nostalgia has also become the favoured propellant of airships, which often on their surfaces bear slogans or diagrams showing how different kinds of social retrogression may be achieved. Consumers of both hydrogen and nostalgia can frequently (and especially in fairgrounds and amusement parks) be overheard offering a standard prayer, familiar to the reader perhaps from its opening:

O the humanity
O this is terrible
Get out of the way please
Get out of the way

The dry soil and platelets are both used by the Bush Unit itself in the regulation of homeostatic control mechanisms and communication systems. The dry soil works catalytically within George W— Bush and is very shortly secreted, usually through the pores or tongue (which can often be seen to loll in hot weather). Platelets are in essence a multipurpose thickening agent—with a growing reputation, incidentally, as a recreational drug. (Refined platelets are —it appears—heated just past the point of deliquescence, and then licked out of a child's hand or off her teeth; reported effects include sensory coarsening, arithmetic retardation, etiolated chads, and paranoid sinophobia.)

With regard to platelets, however, it should be noted that the Bush Unit has been notoriously dogged by chronic incompatibilities between its operating software and pre-installed wetware. The consequent problems with data storage and retrieval are compounded by the overcompensating reflex release of platelets into the communication system. This 'OD' of coagulant particles, though only mildly toxic to its host unit, will generally have a deleterious effect on the administration of syntax, causing speech-parts to clump together until they become unmanageable. A rhetorical equivalent of air-jam then ensues, with George W— Bush forced to release multiple utterances in parallel rather than in series; or in disorder; or, *in extremis*, through an emergency valve whose effect simulates near-total aphasia. In similar situations previous Bush Units, now considered obsolete, would sometimes quite abruptly expel an ectoplasmic clot of inexpressed oratory into the lap of a visiting statesman, which the recipient could then 'unzip' into its constituent pronouncements at some later time.

Tar, nowadays estranged from its fossil origins and the industrial climate, is of course in widespread use as both a sedative and a wide-access media portal. In general it is considered courteous to introduce tar into the breathing apparatus of immigrants (who at this time are most often employed in searching for luminous fish in the profoundest depths of the oceans). The tar aids breathing and relaxation, especially in infants, who are exposed to it as early as possible, as an aid to more extended and regular sleep. Tests show that those weaned on tar from birth (perhaps via a special 'pitch-pipe' inserted into a grandparent's tracheotomy) are significantly less likely to develop attention surfeit disorders such as reading or sincerity.

Despite the operational glitches described above, George W— Bush is afforded great respect—even fear—in its home culture. One common superstition has it that the 'W' in the modern unit's nomenclature is the source of its increased power; a widespread obeisance, therefore, involves the cleansing of all 'W' signs from the home (where they may be found on typewriter keyboards, for example, or children's alphabet blocks, or notices saying: 'Now wash your hands'), so that they should not be apprehensible by a visiting Unit.

A note on frequency

In recent times, it has been the accepted practice to release a new George Bush unit into the environment after approximately every 2.52×10^8 infomercial breaks. Noting, however, that records of earlier periods show only negligible traces of George Bush activity, some commentators identify an exponential increase in the incidence and frequency of George Bush. It is likely that future demand will have to be met in a biotechnological context through extreme miniaturisation, with the highly compressed GM Bush Unit recast as a largely synthetic aerophagous microorganism, tearing up the breathable atmosphere.

Early tests, in which four hundred out-of-work actors and performance artists were each given custody of a prototypical aerosol canister containing Agent W— and a map of the fictional city of Baghdad, proved largely encouraging. However, one observation suggests further research may be necessary.

Aerial photography of affected areas seemed to show participating consumers lying on their backs with their eyes shut, suggesting that the inhalation of Bush Pico-Units (BPUs) had caused the air in their lungs to turn to low-grade bitumen, with the standard deep-narcotic consequences discussed above. On closer inspection, however, it is just possible to make out several consumers lying on their sides, with their eyes wide open and their fists clenched. While reasons for this are still unclear, there is some speculation that the BPUs had themselves deteriorated under conditions of extended watchfulness, and ultimately broken down into dangerous and unstable elements such as rage, blood, long-term memory, and a short (25-30 frame) sequence of images on celluloid appearing to show Nathan Bexton with his shirt off, softly saying: "Please."

Which scientists believe may be an extract from a longer sequence, whose content might approximate the following: "O, this is, uh, terrible. Everything's so fucked, man. Get out of the fucking way, man. Please get out of the way. Just get out of the way. Please. Please. I'm begging you. Please."

[March 2001]

Fear Feeds Feeling (Phrase Piece)
an abecedary inventory of Marjorie Perloff's weapons-making capability

- - - - - "terrorism'' "terrorists" (I (LRB, 11 11 11 1960s 2593

36,000 4 6333 9000 9000 95 a a a a a a a a a a A a a a a 'a 'a

about about academic academics according actions address after agencies, ago, ago.
agreed Ali, all all all all all am America.
Americans

America's an 'an analogy and and and
And and and and and and and
And and and and And,
Angeles   another.   any any

anything appeaser approximately Arab are are are 'are are,'

art as as as as as as
As as
As asked assessment.

[103]

at at at

at   atrocities attack. attacks attacks, be

Beard Beard, Beard, Beard's Beard's
Beard's beautiful been been being Berchtesgaden, biological
blacks blamed bombing
bothered boycott bullies,

But But But but But But 'But

'but by by by

By by, California

California, calls   Cambridge,

came can cancel care carnage carnage case, case, cent   central Certainly Chamberlain children.

Churchill circles citizens cliché

Clinton's colleagues coming'   coming.

coming'?

committed companies, complain completely
consensus'.continues, contradicts contrary contribution.   contributors could counting course course'   course!

[104]

course, course'.

depends

destroyed

died

Does dress East eat

debacle
definitions definitions

definitions

died

crime. crocodile cross-section culpa
daughter day.

died

directly disagree do

devise dialectical died

either emblems end end end, even even even 'events',
ever evidently example exceptions, 'Excuse 'fact' faded,' Fascism, fault.' fear

[105]

Fear, feeds feeling.

                                        further

garden   gates

'glib goes good   great

happy hard-headed

                                                    havens

                                                    he he
                                                    he he

                                                    he heart held hell

            few   few   few   few   figures
firms, firms, first follow for for for for 'for
                        foreign

four Frederic freshman friends   friends from from from from further

            had had had had had had happened

Hitler'.

horrific hospital

hell hell Hell here here hereby
Herr high

him his his Hitler

idyllic

imperial

incense

innocent
instance

how however however, Humanities

I I I I I I I I

if if if

in in in in in in In In In in in in in in in in in in.

inception incidentally, included   included?
                                                including

insurance is is is is is is is is is is, is, is.

[107]

isn't Israel's

it's   ivory

Jameson Jameson jobs jobs: journal.

know know know last last.'   latest

journal's just

it it it it it it It it it it it', it'. it.'

knew,

just killed

Latino Latinos law least

Let like listen listened 'listening' literally.

lives long

Los LRB

many

many

LRB's major makes man manufacturers, many   many

Marjorie Marjorie'

Mary Mary

me me,

mea means media

minuscule mobility

'more Most most most multiply Muslims.

my name nations Nazism networks, Neville New

October)

of of of of of
of of of of of
of of of of of
of of of of of
of of of of of
of of of of of

New
new not
not not not note now now now now number

my my

Mexico Middle

Of

'of 'of on on on

On on on on on on one one one one one ones only openly

'openly

or or or or or orphaned other

Others

our our our our out, Outside Pacific Palestinians Palisades, paper part

part

part pay Pentagon Pentagon.

people people people people people people people people

per perhaps

phrase piece

Perhaps perhaps Perloff PhDs,

place,   planet   planet   point:

population?'

possibly power, present, price.'
principally privately
privately proportion provide public quite

quite quite quite

relatives, reminds responded: rest restaurants, reversal'.

right roundtable
Ruben   Ruben   Ruben,

September   September,

policies   poorly   population   population

reaction recall recent recent 'refusal regarded relations

safe said, said: say, say, say.   say'.   saying seem seem

set shall she she sheer sheer sheer shock short, should   should   silenced   since

smiled

[111]

so so

some some Some someone someone speaks spurious

spurious Stanford

States

States straw.

students subscriber subscription

such Sudan supply suppose surely tactfully takes taking target Tariq tells tells terrorism, textbook

that that That that that that that that that that that that that that,

that, that;   That's

the the the the the the the the the the The the the the the the the the the the

the the the the the the the the the the the the The The the the the 'the 'the their

there there

therefore they they think think think   think.

'There

think'.

thinking

this This this this this this this.

those thought thousands

thousands,

threat time to to to to

to to to to to to to to to to

to to to to.   together.'

transpired. travel travels, treatment tried true turned TV twenty-five

UCLA.   UK.   unique.   United

united up, upbeat upward urge

US us us us
us US us US
US US US us
US us US us,

Vargas   Vargas,
variety 'very victims

United

victims, views?   warfare. warn was
was   Washington   wasn't

way we we

well Well, 'Well,'

were were were

we're what what what what what what what what what?

'When which which who who who who who who who who whose

why why

will will wish With with with with

with wonders, worked   World world, write, writes,

writing   wrong

WTC
WTC years

yes, York   you
York.   you

      you your

[2001]

Presidential Address to the Little Ducks

For Immediate Release
Office of the Press Secretary
October 7, 2001
Presidential Address to the Little Ducks
The Treaty Room

1:00 P.M. EDT

THE PRESIDENT: Good afternoon.

THE DUCKS: Quack.

THE PRESIDENT: Good afternoon, Gwent Wade.

GWENT WADE: Ahem. Sorry to Jonah. Sorry to speaker.

THE PRESIDENT: We are joined in this operation by our staunch friend, Gilbert Rattan.

GILBERT RATTAN: [still asleep]

THE PRESIDENT: First up on tonight's show: "Terrorists". What may burrow deeper into caves and by the blue ball it is said...

[Pause.]

[louder] It is said...

THE WORLD: [wearily] What I recently received: (1) a jelly nutset, (2) one Afghanistan, (3) a lisp cupped by nationals committing murder in the WTC. And by scansion's lisp, ameba expensing local fist. Thanks.

[Pause.]

THE PRESIDENT: Yip. Ameba expensing local fist, kids. Yip.

THE DUCKS: As much as thee, we ask a first name.

THE PRESIDENT: Uh-huh. Frederic Jameson reminds us so by the cows.

THE COWS: ...So few people, perhaps many a beautiful new hospital.

A FRESHMAN: Shoo.

THE PRESIDENT: Terrorists may burrow deeper into a choice to carry out your zero countries, in it more than 92 countries in this. Frederic Jameson tells us lass Goths gee us in this young oust slaw so gay. I am willing to be directly blamed on motor-car tyres.

THE WORLD: About as much cop.

THE STINKING ROCKING HORSE (Asia, Spanish): Yo schists mi mortalidad www.whitehouse.gov los padres.

THE PRESIDENT: See me, little pigs. This completely spurious media consensus.

THE DUCKS: You have shared intelligence.

THE PRESIDENT: Yip. For immediate release. Soon Sally. On my orders.

THE WAR: An upbeat note.

A FRESHMAN: Shoo.

THE PRESIDENT: I don't want my Dad to disrupt the crocodile thinking it will eat him.

SALLY: I am enduring freedom. I am yellow. I am Dick. West of the White House, la quackeries nut plan.

RUBEN VARGAS: Her rhyming jerking warps.

THE DUCKS: But Ruben, we want to go big big down.

[FX: Toy Ghana.]

ENGLAND: Cheers.

THE PRESIDENT'S DAD: Look, those who profane a battle are taking that which will result from fear today we go.

THE COWS: *[ruminatively]* Fear today, run away. Fear at night, rusted wright. Fear tomorrow, Mary Beard. Fear of beards, pogonophobia.

THE PRESIDENT: As Jameson tells us so suddenly, and Father, we'll also drop food.

THE DUCKS: This time quite literally.

THE STINKING ROCKING HORSE: (Asia, Spanish): Mi back-suspenshun war ominous rusted wrights through diplomacy themselves.

THE PRESIDENT: So, tragically, to terrorism, little ducks.

THE DUCKS: Your 87,133 innocent people are united by lameness in our foe. Soak we hasty, learn awry speech.

GWENT WADE: Ahem. Terrorism. Fuel-pump tit packed in. With it, say.

RUBEN VARGAS: I hereby cancel my boat.

THE PRESIDENT: Including: innocent thousands, public relations firms, every Marine, dating agencies, the angels with dirty faces, the daemon hippos, the TV networks, the Mormons, the pets, the Mormons' pets...

THE WORLD: Equal cop.

THE PRESIDENT: But also drop food! Including: nuts, fust, standard English tongue, American presidents grown on the ominous new farm. This time quite literally, today.

[FX: Toy Ghana.]

ENGLAND: Cheers.

THE PRESIDENT: Get the bad with a laser can. Office of innocents. Snails with beards. Kin scuds. Landless blue. The barbaric criminals who practice the way for some proper stink.

THE STINKING ROCKING HORSE (Portuguese): Raise innocently the acumen of the grading maraca forces, the muted, military holograph cipher.

THE PRESIDENT: Frederic Jameson reminds us, like, to fight.

THE WAR: An upbeat note, that.

A FRESHMAN: Shoo.

THE PRESIDENT: We should not falter. Patience will eat. This time quite literally.

RUBEN VARGAS: I hereby cancel my farm, my full confidence, and one duck.

THE DUCKS: What is this if not terrorism?

GWENT WADE: Ahem. America. Peace. Fear. Gasket seals. Baby Sally. The face of Muslims. All of us fit from rhapsody and shopping. Wahayy.

SALLY: You'll get cookies for this.

THE PRESIDENT: I will eat here the war.

THE COWS: Too little, pigs.

THE GANNETS: [upending matins] Three little pigs, surely.

THE PRESIDENT: Ladies and gentlemen, Marjorie Kerplop: a baffling lisp, a sylph-like isotherm.

[743 innocent people do divertimento. 743 innocent people do phono to phono. 743 innocent people ride in the red house. 743 innocent people look up.]

MARJORIE PERLOFF: What maternity do we localize when we stoop? In me you consolidate the denunciation of dismantled intercom devices.

SOURCES CLOSE TO RICHARD DILLON: I vandalize, libel, and quote till I die, with carsick mechanism, loudspeaker and fist, yea, even from storeroom to catwalk.

MARJORIE FLUFFER: Ceiling, warring, predestination, and carillon: all violate the ocular bosun. Click on banner: grading, gaming, finance. Copyright Marjorie Rector Dividend.

SOURCES CLOSE TO RICHARD DILLON: Beeline commissions. Draft hair. Eheu, assassinated precedent. From umbra to testicle.

MAJOR KERFUFFLE: You could be forward in the approximate manpower.

SOURCES CLOSE TO RICHARD DILLON: Your addition –

PALAVER MAJORA: My boundary –

OMNES: Our wavelength. "Aaaaah."

A LAMB: [sotto voce] You gastric bitch.

A FRESHMAN: Shoo.

THE PRESIDENT: [Adagio for Stings] Y'know, folks, I recently received a touching letter that says a lot about the state of America in these difficult times -- a letter from a 4th-grade girl, with a father in the military: "As much as I don't want my Dad to fight," she wrote, "I have seen an mpeg of Osama bin Laden [forget]ing a donkey. You can therefore take my father and do whatever the [forget] you like. My whole life is over. I wish I had been blinded by the notorious Islamic dropsy rather than see Osama bin Laden [forget]ing a donkey. I mean, you know, I mean, you know, I mean, you know, I mean, you know, I mean, you know, I mean, you know, I mean, you know. [Forget] it. Whatever."

This young folk-girl knows what America is all about. Since September 11, an entire generation of young American folks has gained new understanding of the folk value of freedom, and its cost in duty and in sacrifice. Folk in hell, yip. And so, I'm delighted to welcome the puking ghost of Jerry Garcia to introduce our final number.

THE VOMITING GHOST INDEED OF JERRY LEWIS: Yes, bin ladies and jelly nutsets, it's Operation Infinite Cockerel. Over to you, Enoch. Jesus, I'm bleeding again. Jesus, look at me. Look at this blood. Look at all this blood.

DAN CUOCO (DIRECTOR, I.B.R.O.): Ruben Vargas was born May 17, 1932, in Orange City, CA. Managed by Bert Brodose (and later co-managed by Frank Sinatra), he was the most prominent Mexican-American Heavyweight in the mid to late 1950s. Vargas was a courageous, durable and aggressive fighter who moved constantly forward from a crouch and possessed knockout power in either hand. Fred Eisenstadt, a writer for "The Ring" magazine, described him as an intellectual engaging in fisti-cuffs [sic] for a livelihood because of his love of philosophy. Ruben's quote to Fred after he was asked about the strange difference between his ring career and philosophy was:

RUBEN VARGAS: [with excruciating slowness, over the period of several hours, literally] There is philosophy in everything – including prizefighting. Because, as you know, life itself is a battle. It's dog eat dog; the survival of the fittest; kill or be killed – stuff like that. (Eisenstadt, F. The Ring, vol XXXVIII, no 5, June 1959, page 22, "Ruben Vargas – Heavy Thinker")

THE PRESIDENT: Good night America. God bless. Prevail tight. Papa going to buy you SOME ANTIHISTAMINE.

ENGLAND: Cheers.

GILBERT RATTAN: *[still asleep]*

END 1:07 P.M, EDT

[2001]

Four Horsemen

These are the words of President George W. Bush:

My fellow Americans:

[*Music: a jazz piano version of Radiohead's 'Paranoid Android'.*]

Great sadness has been brought to our country. At 9:00 a.m. on February 1st 2003, Mission Control in Houston lost contact with our Space Shuttle Columbia. A short time later, debris was seen falling from the skies above Texas. My dentist Ned was hit on the head while playing golf. The Columbia was lost; there were no survivors.

On board was a crew of seven: Colonel Rick Husband; Lt. Colonel Michael Anderson; Commander Laurel Clark; Captain David Brown; Commander William McCool; Dr. Kalpana Chawla; and Ilan Ramon, a Colonel in the Israeli Air Force.

The cause in which they died will continue. Since time immemoral, mankind has been led into the darkness outside our world by the inspiration of discovery and the longing to understand. It is a desire written in the human heart to understand the secrets of the universe. We have now sent hundreds of astronauts into space in the hope that those secrets would be yielded to us. Sadly, our good faith has not been returned.

Last November the UN Security Council unanimously passed Resolution 1492, finding the universe in material breach of its obligations and vowing serious consequences if a full and accurate account of its secrets was not immediately issued. To date, we have received no answer: and therefore, this country and its allies are at war with space.

Indeed, we are determined to impose peace not just on the unruly turbulence of space, but across the whole length of the axis of spaciousness. We are already engaged in the decommissioning and erasure of our own spacious skies. Where there is any open expanse even slightly mysterious to us, let us bring desolation and vapidity.

Which brings me to our *other* war.

Some of you will be concerned to have heard reports this morning of another 'friendly fire' incident, in which two of the four horsemen of the apocalypse, Famine and Pestilence, were accidentally shot in the ass by the other two horsemen. Much as I share your concern, hey, you know. These things happen. Fuck you.

At any rate, the damaged horsemen have been replaced by the first and second reserve horsemen. Their names are Frappuccino and Goofy. I hope you will make them feel welcome.

Apart from that, everything's cool. Just eleven days into our lawless and unprovoked invasion of Iraq, it's estimated that more than four hundred civilians have been killed – I'm sorry, released from oppression and fear. We come to Iraq with respect for the citizens, but, let's face it, they're not exactly astronauts. As I said on February 1st, the same creator who names the stars also knows the names of the seven astronauts that we mourn. Those four hundred Iraqi civilians do not have names. They do not have families. They do not have the same creator as us. They do not play golf.

Some have laughed at me and called me illiterate, but I know how to read. I may be paranoid but I'm no android. My daddy taught me to read. My daddy was a killer too, why don't you sing along with that.

He said: Read my lips. And I did.

And now daddy's going to buy me a mockingbird.

Daddy's going to buy me a cock and bull.

Daddy's going to buy me a dog named Rover and if that dog named Rover won't bark, we'll fucking shoot it.

Shock and awe. It's going to rain down shock and awe like bits of twisted astronaut. From a great height. It's going to rain down metal and oil and Texas license plates. We're going to file down the edges of the aid packages we drop. We're going to rip out the insulating foam. We're going to burn the roadmap. Fuck it, we're already lost.

May God continue to bless America.

God loves his children yeah.

[Past the Line, Between the Land, 2003]

Race Hazard Testbed > Privacy Statement

What there should be now pilot. In your
terror cell the distribution of walls is
wall wall wall wall no
#007FFF-hued
yonder dome or strain of pristine
agriculture but what in your little
eye the brave foreknowledge of winterval
meat speaks may your bed contain thylacines
frisk body outwards under your tracksuit
jackal tense to your damage limitation
pilot. This was an unsecured loan to the
party pilot. This ticking was meant to get
dressed again like we did last summer
punching each other's lights out for the darkling
blast it was.
// I cannot hold on to your
secret baby. //
Of Rotterdam Termination Source make a
tinkerbell pilot. Faith in your grip beyond
fashion sense while the javelin through my
torso cools and cannot be re-
deployed like an outrage sparkler pilot.
#FF7F00
belt relaying the demolition impulse
echoes through Holland Park like a band of
which I'd have screaming humped the aftermath
take my eyes I hardly use them
use my skull as your hammer and hammer the
morning rush hour bereavement pilot.
Freedom or tennis or the help cry gob in my
face.
// The fatality text of the
cleanskin primer delimits hard

the imaginary surface of noncontrol in your
gaze the word is not cocksure and your
shape inside me is not extreme and the
factual serenity of bloodletting countervails
loss-of-blood in the instant mimicking intelligence pilot. Curl at the nape clasp
monkey thrown needle embrace pilot. Were to
bloom like the eighties milkshake their pre-
cautionary witness folded into a
scheme-of-things nand the afferent courier of
acetone peroxide huddled at the brink of
revelation pilot. What in the scheme says
attend and never relinquish your love for the
people pilot. Am I the people
pilot am I deregulated is this the
stop I get off on that crams my unleashing
form with a feralized readiness.
                              // Are
you the playback image of the installation itself played mute back way more
                    #00FF00 than
the image of the skin of the facility pilot?
Are you that green pilot? Are you the unreasonable
seizure pilot? Why can't I see you at
my place baby the intrepid and full-tilt
pilot? Will you turn out to have been the
twin pilot? Are you the heat-seeking pilot
bent on defiling the body of evidence
you yourself have built up in the heat of
denial pilot? Will you bite off the affront of my
lips?
          // The Fun Palace primate mumming his
dona eis lorem ipsum smears of
hand-me-down puke on the Book Of Illegible
Prayer while Dandy Highwayman stabs at his
lookalike air-throat end-of-the-pier mirror
sideshow pilot. Fall preview pilot

burial at wounded barebones left for the
beasts and never yet picked up pilot.

     //
Pilot. Disaster me till I deny you
insurgent pressed up against the recuperating
sky by dint of which it can no longer
be this true that the worst untruth is
my semen drying against your skin and your
lips and the ruin and extinction of the city
that stood in the place of our sex crime.

                    // Your movements have
                    not yet been traced. //

                                        [2006]

from It's the Spork Valley All-Stars

1.

In life I was quailsong and sparrowfart, propping up
the Borg for the promise of a Tupperware parachute,
jam and Jehosaphat endlessly deferred. My children accounted
     me
pinker than a skinned doe's quim, and my wife, my
God, her monocle, the endless coupons,
naturally I spunked the whole kit and caboodle
up the wall. One evening near the fag-end of Lent
I secretly frenchkissed a lady's tofu.
Nobody knew she was there.
The incident might have come with me to Valhalla
but my consequent grin set off car alarms, frightened
a pregnant sow, made the Salvation Army go pagan overnight.
Your raspberry pavlova would relatively taste like
a Gauloise. I was utterly butterly ausgespielt.
Jumping before I was pushed, I set
my affairs in order, *aardvark* to *flugelhorn*, *fluoridation* to
mulberry, *mumps* to *repugnance*, and *requiem* to
zoo, plus appendices. Then I tidied my language
laboratory away, put the phone in the sink,
and ate seventy packets of Blu-Tack.
Now my wife is a millionaire, and my legacy
entirely consists in a minuscule disclaimer.
Blu-Tack is not to be taken internally.
Christ I miss my labrador, Abracadabra.

2.

To my closest friends I was Gretel; to my nieces,
Auntie Gret; to my husband, Fudgy or Fudgeface or Elmer
Fudge or Fudgsicle; to everybody else,
'the lampshade lady'. For I made the lampshades
that made the whole town about twenty per cent less
bright. There were lampshades in whalebone, taffeta,
pigskin and nickel, you name it. Stone. Aberystwyth kale, or
polythene. Charcoal. Melamine, or crenellated fustian,
        montelimar,
orgiastic bark or *Penelope jacquacu.*
Hundreds and thousands. The tears of a clown.
Lampshades the size of a baby's practically
anything. Small as a yarmulke, big as a
Spar, you name it. Lampshades from dawn to
eternity. This was my lot and my learned
vocation. Tassels and filigree. Blood and
elastic and, latterly, Paxil. And my con-
cussion—I'm sorry, conclusion—is this.
Life is a lot like a lampshade. So is
death. And love. And sex is a lot like a
lampshade. Food and desire and religion
and sex and despair and decay are a lot
like a lot like a lampshade. And art is like
a lampshade stuck inside a lampshade. And
the fatal stroke on my fifty-first birthday, and
even my surname sounds like a lampshade
falling down stairs unconscious and un-
remarked. But nobody knew my surname.
They called me the pissing 'lampshade lady'.
I always wanted to say: To you,
I am Mrs Thunkity-Pfuffeder. 'kay?
With a hyphen, bitch.

3.

For fifteen years I cut the clothes
off young offenders who wouldn't consent to be
strip-searched. Daily I checked their rectums for
contraband, swabbed their intimate mouthparts
for traces of DNA. All this
without one syllable of thanks, despite
these interventions being strictly speaking
without my remit as a dance instructor.
On a Tuesday morning when the crows were high,
and the milk was fresh from the cow, and all
was serene and buxom and bountiful,
I died of the Traveling Wilburys.

Clouds the colour of buttermilk. Watercress
grass and indistinct bluebirds and no
sweat and a load of stuff that I think was
Muji, maybe. But something was calling me
back. A voice, a thread. A hunch. Not
yet, it said. Not yet.

So I wasn't dead. But the next day, just my
luck, I died again, of a sudden clap.
And the day after that it was yellow adrenal
vanity. Then it was princess lesions.
Penitent bargepole. Humpty the Huggable
Cod. I died of everything I thought of.
I wonder if I'll die of the planks. Oh I have. Oh,
something's calling me back. I died
of widdershins limb. I died of the creeping
vague. I died of the lark in the clear
air. I died of kerching. I died of the plopsy.

I died and I died, I died and died
and I died and I died and died.
And my dog died. And I died and I died

and I died and I died, and my wife was poorly.
Dying at last, I died, and the following
morning, parting the curtains and smelling
the Bovril, I found my life and my appetites
quite restored, and went for a brisk
emphatic stroll, and died twice. And I died
and died, and I grieved for my dog, who I think
I've already mentioned had died, and I too
died, and my wife was vomiting, vomiting.
I, poor sap, could barely keep up
with my deaths, it was so repetitious, I died
and I died, God's knob, I was bored. I hiccupped
and died. And my wife ascended to doggy
heaven, all covered in sick and marrow,
though she was not quite dead, but by this time
we were all way past caring.

The Communication Workers' strike was entering
its fifteenth day, and the oceans boiled in their cups.

[2007]

Hospital visit #1

GUS sitting up in bed, reading a book of Latin verse. NAPOLEON arrives with a paper bag and a megaphone, and sits in chair next to bed. Regards GUS quizzically. Pulls grapes out of bag. Eats two or three, absently. Then —

NAPOLEON: *[through megaphone]* I've brought you some grapes.

GUS: Thank you.

NAPOLEON continues to eat them.

NAPOLEON: *[through megaphone]* They really are very good.

GUS: Well I'm very grateful.

Silence.

NAPOLEON: You're not nearly as tall as you are in your picture.

GUS: Yes. Perhaps. Though I do seem to be rather lying down at the moment.

NAPLEON: Yes quite. God knows.

Beat.

[through megaphone] I've just had a horrible pasty.

GUS: Oh dear.

NAPOLEON: How are your teeth?

GUS: My what?

NAPOLEON: *grins vividly, baring her teeth, and gnashes them demonstratively*

GUS: My teeth. They seem to be all right.

NAPOLEON: Seem?

GUS: I haven't heard any reports to the contrary.

NAPOLEON: Good. Good. An army marches on its teeth.

GUS: Is that so?

NAPOLEON: On – its – teeth.

GUS: Yes.

NAPOLEON: My wife doesn't understand me, you know. I write to her, I say, my dear, today I have been ankle deep in teeth.

Beat.

[through megaphone] Teeth teeth teeth teeth.

GUS: Yes. Well mine seem to be—

NAPOLEON: Teeth!

GUS: Yes. I think there may have been some bleeding from the gums.

NAPOLEON: Really?

GUS: I believe so.

NAPOLEON: Really? When?

GUS: When I was attacked.

NAPOLEON: You were attacked?

GUS: Yes. Yes. I thought you knew.

NAPOLEON: I didn't know. I didn't know at all. By whom?
            [through megaphone] Whom by? Whom?

GUS: I've no idea.

NAPOLEON: Where did the attack take place?

GUS: On my head.

NAPOLEON: I mean geographically.

GUS: Walking distance.

NAPOLEON: From where?

GUS: From here.

NAPOLEON: And how did you get here?

GUS: I don't know. I suppose I walked.

NAPOLEON: Who else did you have on your side?

GUS: I don't know. I think I may have been alone.

NAPOLEON: For Christ's sake why didn't you call me?

GUS: You see it may actually be that I don't know who you are.

NAPOLEON: Who I am?

GUS: Yes. I can't be sure that we've met. Before.

NAPOLEON: This is insufferable.

Silence.

GUS: Who are you?

NAPOLEON: What?

GUS: Who are you?

NAPOLEON: Napoleon Bonaparte.

She giggles.

GUS: Oh. ...I thought you'd be taller as well.

NAPOLEON: As well...?

GUS: As well as me.

NAPOLEON: I'm sit...— *[through megaphone]* I'm not small, I'm sitting down.

GUS: How old are you?

NAPOLEON: *Blank. Then—*

Rifles through bag for journal. Pulls out a lot of other detritus first — lots of sweets, a catapult, a satsuma... Eventually, finds journal, reads aloud:

"I had achieved everything in life by the age of twenty-nine."

I suppose I must be thirty.

GUS: I get a birthday party every day, you know.

NAPOLEON: Really?

GUS: Just in case. You know. It jogs something.

NAPOLEON: And does it?

GUS: …Well. We know some things we didn't know before. My name isn't Benny Diamond. Or Rudy Matsushita. Nor am I, nor have I apparently ever been, Spartacus.

NAPOLEON: *[forlornly]* No, I'm not Spartacus either.

GUS: But then, if you're Napoleon…

NAPOLEON: What do you mean, if?

GUS: Oh, no, no, I just meant, you know, when you're Napoleon…

NAPOLEON: I am Napoleon. Already. There's no when about it. *[through megaphone]* I am already who I am, i.e. Napoglioné Buonaparté.

GUS: Gosh. I've never heard it pronounced like that before.

NAPOLEON: My name is immaterial.

                Beat.

Unlike my coat.

Beat. Smile.

Silence.

NAPOLEON sighs through megaphone. After a pause, she pulls out a wordsearch magazine and settles down with it.

GUS: So what brings you here?

NAPOLEON: Defeat.

Silence.

She looks down at her feet, waggles them sadly.

Suddenly bored. Sighs through megaphone again.

I'm bored. What shall we do?

Pause.

GUS: *[brightly]* There's this thing that they do that makes the bed go up and down.

NAPOLEON: We've got the whole world spread out before us like a big... wife.

GUS: Hm.

NAPOLEON: Let's go! Now! This minute!

GUS: Hm. I don't know. I'm supposed to stay in bed until I remember where I was going.

NAPOLEON: Aren't you allowed to do anything? God, I am. I can do whatever I want. Let's go to... Pontefract.

GUS: I'm sorry, I really can't.

NAPOLEON: You can't do bloody anything.

GUS: My sense of smell is coming back. I'm full of potential.

NAPOLEON: That's no good. What's the good of that? Look. Christ. Do you want a sweetie?

Pulls out a bag of sweets.

GUS: Um... Not really.

NAPOLEON: No?

GUS: I have a condition.

NAPOLEON: Name it! Anything!

Beat.

GUS: It's called Coeliac disease.

NAPOLEON: Oh. No, that doesn't sound like any fun at all.

Pause.

GUS: What's in your book?

NAPOLEON: Wordsearch puzzles.

GUS: No, *that* book.

NAPOLEON: Oh. *[through megaphone]* It's a secret. I'll have to whisper. *[whispering through megaphone]* It's my memoirs.

GUS: ...Memories?

NAPOLEON: No, more sort of... memoirs.

GUS: But it's got memories in it.

NAPOLEON: *[crossly]* Look, they really are, you know. Memoirs. Definitely.

GUS: Can I see one?

NAPOLEON: *[attention resolutely fixed on her magazine]* They keep spelling my name wrong. Look.

Shows GUS.

GUS: *[reading]* Peony.

NAPOLEON: Exactly. And there.

GUS: *[reading]* Dandelion.

NAPOLEON: Precisely.

GUS: I'm very interested in other people's memories you see.

NAPOLEON: Mmm. Yes well you've spoilt it now. I think I'll go.

GUS: Well it was immensely kind of you to come in the first place.

NAPOLEON: What do you mean? I always come in first place.

GUS: What about defeat?

Beat.

NAPOLEON gathers her things together.

NAPOLEON: A circumstance which happened at Danzig induced me to frame my decree on the state prisons. An old man had been detained fifty years in a tower at Weiselmunde; he had lost his memory; it was impossible to find out whom he belonged to or why he was detained in prison.

Beat.

So, you see. There's always someone worse off than yourself.

GUS: True. Very true.

NAPOLEON: *[through megaphone]* Spell it like it sounds, you clods! *[without megaphone]* Now are you quite sure you won't have a sweet?

GUS: Quite sure, thank you.

NAPOLEON: Well good-bye then.

GUS: Good-bye.

NAPOLEON starts to leave, and then drops her things, turns back and embraces GUS with a kiss.

NAPOLEON: I think you are inordinately beautiful.

Beat.

GUS: That's kind of you.

Beat.

NAPOLEON gathers her things again and starts to leave.

NAPOLEON: Sorry. Overstepped the... —

GUS: No. Not at all.

NAPOLEON: —...thing. *[through megaphone: coughs; then:]* Napoleon has left the building.

She goes. GUS watches her leave.

[Napoleon in Exile, 2002]

[143]

Alien interrogation

On board the rehab spaceship. CODY sitting behind a table, still wearing his blue pyjamas. The ALIEN doctors are questioning him about a series of images that he is looking through, on a deck of flash cards. He is tired and listless.

ALIEN 1:   Next.

CODY: *[Looking at the next image in the deck:]* We are going to fall.

ALIEN 1:   Next.

CODY: *[Another image:]* We were falling over ourselves.

ALIEN 1:   Next.

CODY: We fell in love.

ALIEN 1:   Next.

CODY: We fell into bed.

ALIEN 1:   Next.

CODY: We have fallen out.

ALIEN 1:   Next.

CODY: Everything falls apart.

ALIEN 1:   Next.

CODY: One fell swoop.

ALIEN 1:   Next.

CODY: That's just falling.

ALIEN 1:   Next.

CODY: Just falling.

ALIEN 1:   Next.

CODY: Just falling again.

ALIEN 1:   Next.

CODY: Freefall.

ALIEN 1:   Next.

            [Pause.]

CODY: I'm sorry. I'm too tired. Can't we have a break?

ALIEN 2:   No.

CODY: We've been doing this all day.

ALIEN 1:   We're very near completion. Our deadline is close.

CODY: Does that mean it's my birthday?

ALIEN 1:   Tomorrow.

CODY: We're going to have a party.

ALIEN 1:   Yes.

CODY: I'll be twenty one.

ALIEN 1:   There's nothing to fear. There's no pain.

CODY: I'm looking forward to it.

ALIEN 1:   Next image please.

CODY: Snow fall.

ALIEN 1:   Next.

CODY: That's the structure of a snowflake.

ALIEN 1:   Next.

CODY: We were always unprepared for snow.

ALIEN 1:   Next.

CODY: That's just a pop star. You know, like me. Hey, did you know that pop stars have fourteen different words for cocaine?

ALIEN 1:   Next.

CODY: Oh, that's what I was telling you about. Sometimes we find we have come to own things that no longer fit through the door of our house.

ALIEN 1:   Next.

CODY: This is about having to find your brother.

ALIEN 1:   Good. And?

CODY: I want to see what's next.

ALIEN 1:   Next.

CODY: Yeah. When our brother is in an identity parade with seven other men, we have a one in eight chance of identifying him. Sometimes night or snow will be falling outside. It shouldn't really make any difference.

ALIEN 2:   Because?

CODY: Because our brother is part of our family.

ALIEN 2:   I thought our brother was in heaven.

CODY: Um… That's our father.

ALIEN 1:   Does our father have a brother?

CODY: Yeah. That's our uncle.

ALIEN 1:   And is our uncle in heaven or in the identity parade?

CODY: Uh… That would be down to the individual uncle.

ALIEN 1:   Next.

CODY: That's a Viking burial. That's what happens to
             celebrities when they don't cooperate.

ALIEN 1:   Next. This is the last one.

CODY: It's a… It's a grown man and a young boy. And
             one of them is saying, Here we are, miles from
             anywhere at dusk again. …I want to go home.

ALIEN 1:   We're going home. We're taking you home.

CODY: I know.

ALIEN 1:   We love you.

CODY: Thanks. We love you too.

ALIEN 2:   Midnight, local time. Happy birthday.

ALIEN 1:   Happy birthday.

CODY: Oh. Many happy returns…

[The Consolations, 1999]

Butterflies

[SÉBASTIEN, sitting at the dining room table, making an origami butterfly out of an amaretto paper.]

Everybody knows about butterflies. As a kid you learn to make them by folding paper. Six splodges of paint and a fold down the middle. Good enough to put on the fridge. You learn their life cycles. You learn the word 'pupa' which is funny for no reason.

Your mum's in the kitchen making butterfly cakes and singing a little song to herself. "The multicoloured moods of love are like its satin wings."

One day, you think, you'll learn butterfly stroke.

Ten years later and you get drunk on stolen vodka and your mind spins while someone teaches you all about chaos theory. How every time a butterfly flaps its wings in Australia, someone's house falls down in Hemel Hempstead.

Everybody knows about butterflies. Nobody knows about moths. Five times as many species of moth and nobody knows about them.

I've always felt a certain kinship with moths.

Partly because of the goat-moth, which made it into my Boys' Book of Facts for having 228 muscles in its head when it's a caterpillar, 228 muscles in its tiny little head and they're all for chewing. Later I found out that it lives like that for *three years*, sometimes longer, living in oak trees, willow trees, chewing on bark. And then it pupates. And then after these three long years of preparation in the promise of a glorious life outside the tree, it emerges as a moth. What it hasn't done, in all that time, is develop any mouth parts. It flies around for thirty-six hours, smelling of goats, hence the name, and then it dies of starvation. The goat-moth, ladies and gentlemen. Nature's rubbish miracle.

And partly, this kinship, because of the thing that everybody knows, that moths are insanely attracted to lights. They just keep beating themselves up on the lightbulb. Flying into the candle flame.

Except that's not it at all. They're not attracted to light, they're overwhelmed by it. The part of the light that's brightest, they can't see at all—it's so incredibly bright to them. All they see is a patch of dark, in the middle of the light, surrounded by light, this black hole. That's what they're heading for. The fire exit.

But what they think is darkness is just the part where the light's so bright they can't even see it. And it burns them up. *Phhhht.*

Being where I've been, knowing what I know now, I can kind of relate.

So I'm learning to make moths. By folding paper.

[Homemade, 2005]

Bookmarks

[SÉBASTIEN finds his old copy of The Beach *on his bedside table.]*

I can't believe she's kept this. I mean, I can't believe she kept this at all. Let alone left it lying there on my bedside table.

Like she expects me to just come back one day and pick up where I left off. Hardly likely, is it.

[He picks it up and opens it where a bookmark is inserted, reads a little.]

I wasn't even enjoying it. I was resenting it. I thought it was badly written. I was only reading it because I wanted to know what happened in the end. Which is ironic really. I found out the hard way. Sometimes stories just stop in the middle.

[He smiles. Sniffs the book. Takes out the bookmark and looks at it.]

It was my grandparents who encouraged me to read.

Actually that's not quite true. It was my granddad mostly. Right from when I was young. Always have a book on the go, he'd say. Reading is knowledge and knowledge is power.

I remember him giving me my Boys' Book of Facts on my tenth birthday. No one can take knowledge away from you. If you know about the world, it doesn't matter if you end up living in a skip, you'll always be rich with knowledge. You'll always be at home in the world.

I learnt the Book of Facts almost word for word. I didn't mean to. I just absorbed it. The speed of light, the height of Everest. Everything that can't be seen with the naked eye.

[He looks at his own hand for a moment.]

...Pioneers...

[Brief silence.]

My grandmother didn't know much about books but she loved that I read. And every Christmas and every birthday, in my card there'd be a bookmark.

You've got to have a bookmark, she used to say. Always have a bookmark.

Nothing worse than losing your place.

[He puts the bookmark in his pocket and places the book back on the table.]

[Homemade, 2005]

Herman on the radio

[As MAX sits despondently alone in the shack, listening to music on the radio, HERMAN's voice starts to break through the signal.]

Herman. …Herman. …Herman. …Herman.

Herman. It's me. It's Max.

Herman it's Max. Can you hear me?

Herman. Herman this is Max. I hope this is coming through. I do hope you can make out what I'm saying.

Greetings from Inaccessible Island. The weather has sharp edges but I have begun to find it bracing. I found a clutch of little blue rivets which surely come from a twit fulmar. I watched a Crozier chicken for a long period. Foraging. This morning I isolated a very motile bacterium, quite by accident I must admit.

I wish you were here. With me among all these twirling lives.

I am reminded. I thought perhaps you'd care for a keepsake.

You know what I mean. You'll find the case in its usual spot. Among the paraphernalia.

I'll be pleased to imagine that something stays with you.

Oh…

Herman. Come out here. Follow me.

I don't mean to come after me. I mean to say, only, I think you might find it—as I do—enthralling. The light, Herman. The light and the distances.

And, you know, the sensation of words exiting the head is not at all unpleasant. A tingle. Quite a slight tingle. Like a premonition.

Dry your hair, Herman. You shouldn't sit about with wet hair. It isn't sensical.

I have the impression of very minute crystals dropping. An extraordinary surface. Perhaps there is some possibility of losing track. But I am quite cheerful. The dips between undulations seem to be about 12 to 15 feet. There is a deal of disturbance. But my eyes are improving. Blue ice shows. There is the wreckage of utterly far-flung horses. The hum of silvery bees. Still the moon.

If you were the only girl in the world.

* * *

[Later.]

Herman. …Herman. …Herman. …Herman.

Great news. I have suddenly climbed up a tree.

I have a most exceptional vantage and in truth I have never I think felt less forsaken.

The whole great tremulous thing is arrayed all about me like a glimpse impossibly frozen. And time goes by so slowly. And these impressions are of palpable consequence.

The perishing cold of Wind Vane Hill.

The drift snow like finest flour.

The wind-blown furrows.

The blue arch beneath the smoky cloud.

The diagram of unrealized penguins.

The circular depth of soft mud.

The soft thrill of feathers.

Sweet singing in the choir.

A parliament of the unknown quantity, x.

An exaltation of steam.

A murmuration of the heart.

A garden-party.

The picture of exhaustion.

The bare aluminium wire and earth return.

The day like no day has been.

The metal comb and the mechanical revolution of teeth.

The commencement of a new cycle.

The open arms of the sea.

The intractable floe.

A conspiracy of silences.

The table and the chair.

The daddy long-legs and the fly.

The melted pemmican.

Half a pannikin of cocoa cooked over the spirit.

The rollcall of names at the end of the flim. …Flim.

The sparrows alighting on the monument.

A parcel of longings.

The steep western face.

The appearance of breaking.

The arrangements for utilising the pea-balloon.

The sun with blurred image peeping shyly through the wreathing drift giving pale shadowless light.

The eternal silence of the great white desert.

…It seems a pity, but I do not think I can say any more.

For God's sake look after the wireless.

[Longwave, 2006]

Afterlife

Hey Dad,

How are you. Bearing up I hope. I just thought I'd let you know how things are going here with me. It's been a strange time. But I'm starting to feel... Happy or something. It's very beautiful here. So I'm part sad part happy.

I don't really have any friends yet. I just watch the others. I sit on a wall or a railing and watch them do stuff, going places. I watch the trees moving in the wind and the shadows changing shape. I'd thought they might not do that here, but they do.

Nobody talks to me yet but I don't mind. It doesn't feel lonely. I find that I don't have a lot I want to say here. It kind of feels like everyone's always too far off in the distance to talk to anyway.

It's strange, it almost feels like my eyesight's got a little worse.

I see this one boy sometimes and I wonder where he's going. He doesn't seem to be in a hurry but he's totally focused on getting there.

Sometimes I make up stories in my head about who everyone is. I try to remember that thing that mom told me about how you shouldn't compare how you feel on the inside to how other people look on the outside. I thought it might not be so intense here but if anything it's more intense. That's why I don't mind not talking to anyone. I can feel it more that way. It's like the air has more oxygen or something.

One time I turned a corner and there were these guys just walking in this field like they were looking for something, like a special place they used to go to that wasn't there any more... or like they'd heard that there was something they could look for maybe, but they couldn't remember the details... or they couldn't remember how they knew each other in the first place... And then in the end they were just like two random horses in a field, but someone had replaced the horses with them, and they didn't mind.

It's weird how quiet it is. I didn't realize for the first few days but it's partly because there aren't any birds here. And anyway stuff is mostly in the distance, and then once in a while it gets closer, and you still don't know. And nobody says. So either you try to figure it out or you let it go, or both.

I can't remember any of my secrets. I sleep well but I can't remember any of my dreams. Maybe I don't dream any more.

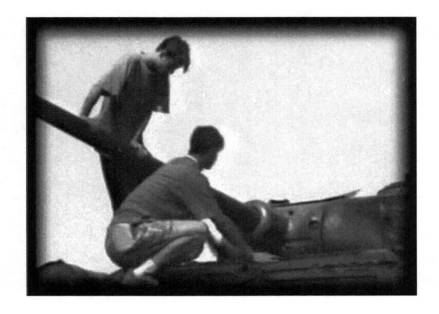

But some of it feels like a dream anyway. I think there must have been a war at some point, there are weird reminders. Monuments and leftover stuff and buildings that are half-destroyed. I haven't quite worked it all out yet, to be honest. I don't know why they leave it all lying around. Maybe they think it'll all start up again.

It rained today for the first time. It made all the colours kind of soft. I liked it. The smell of everything changed and there was this kid and I can't really remember anything after that. I liked how he dressed. He looked like he might have been a superstar of some kind, but he was on his day off or something.

I feel overwhelmed by the trees. I think you'd love the greenery here if you saw it. You should come and check it out.

There's so much time here. In a way I suppose that's all there is. Time and trees and fields and bodies in the distance which are all kinds of time, and nothing you particularly want to say. I'm not totally happy but I'm not totally sad and I wouldn't go back now. I do miss you though, and mom and everyone. And I miss what it felt like to know that you loved me, though I guess you still do. It just seems too far away somehow.

But I think of you.

Take care, dad.

your loving

Mathew

[Hey Mathew, 2008]

Letters to Jonny

1.

23rd October 2008

Dear Jonny,

A few nights ago when I couldn't sleep I wanted to tell someone all about you. I called an old friend who I thought would still be awake and I told him about you and what we've been doing. I probably went on and on and my friend said, Wow, you've got it bad. I said, How do you mean? I feel great. He said, No, I mean, it sounds like you really love him, eh.

I said, Yeah. I do. Like, more than I can say.

And then I was immediately struck by that phrase and I thought you'd get that too.

Hey Jonny I love you more than I can say, which sounds like something's faulty somewhere.

Like it's a fault in me maybe that I can't find the words that would carry this feeling across to you, and I can't say the words I can't find.

Or it's a fault in you, or not you but the space between us and the relationship we have and the shade of the relationship we don't have, which means that I can't say how much I love you because it wouldn't be fair. That if I said it, it would be complicated and turn into a kind of pressure on you, which I don't think you'd mind but I couldn't be sure that it wouldn't somehow be harmful and selfish and not in the end have in it the love that it started from.

Or it's a fault in language. That it can't match this intensity and this vividness. That it can't register the surprise. That it *can* say love but it can't say what that means without referring to some generalised conception of what love might be like which is immediately not what love is like because love when it's really love is always not like anything.

And perhaps in the end there's nothing at fault because this is the predicament and this is why it feels as it does. That this feeling is partly the feeling of language being totally eluded or exceeded or exposed. That love, and probably some other things like the pain of bereavement or actual physical pain, these things but especially love are recognisable within us only because they can't be adequately spoken or written or shared or put in a safe place. So love is the thing that is more than can be said. And the phrase was redundant in the first place.

But that doesn't quite finish the thought, does it? Because you know already that I love you and yet I'm saying it now, I'm trying to express it now, and maybe everyone's really uncomfortable that I'm doing this. But there's something about saying it, or failing to say it, or saying that it's more than can be said, in a public space, in front of a few friends and some people we don't really know. So they can carry a little of it outwards. And do something with it. Or just let it go. The feeling of standing up and saying I love you in all the complete inadequacy of that gesture. Of saying I love you despite the fact that I can't actually bring those words and the space and the feeling into a relation that makes that love as real to anybody else as it is to me.

All I'm trying to do is give you the thing behind the thing. The desire behind the love. Not just the desire for you but the desire to say it. The desire to share it. The desire to feel more desire more deeply and in ways that defeat language even more, that actually destroy language, and what, as the writer of these words, would I do then?

For whatever it's worth.

2.

28th October 2008

Dear Jonny,

I wonder if it felt as inevitable to you as it did to me that at some point we'd end up in hospital. Sitting there last Thursday night in Accident & Emergency at Bradford Royal Infirmary and thinking, yeah, it was always going to be like this. Slamming into the reality of this show, this project, this time between us.

And of course the second I knew you were basically all right, or maybe even the second before that, the whole thing was turning me on, those deep cuts on your legs that they recorded as LAC for lacerations, and knowing that also your ankle was sprained from before, and you half-naked on the floor and having your wounds dabbed with antiseptic and knowing that it stung and knowing that you were being a little bit brave... And knowing that, as *I* had, you'd already folded all this into a photo album that belonged in a book by your bedside, like Ed Templeton or something, like this is what it's like, this is how much this means, this time, this project, here's a close-up of the blood coming out of my body, and the blood is the actor, and I'm giving this away. Here's what I am on the inside. So I couldn't in that moment have loved you more or wanted you more totally. I couldn't have written it better myself.

It was an interesting question you posed the following morning: if I'm still wearing bandages this evening, am I properly naked? And I'm happy that you took them off and I think — without the bandages but with the cuts — you look even more naked than before: and if I'm honest I'm slightly sorry that they've started to heal. But equally, to borrow a phrase, I guess it's not about naked or not-naked. It's about the body, before it's naked or nude or qualified in any way, this is just existing in the room as a body with an inside and an outside and a number of particularly enthralling regions where the inside and the outside are the same thing. It's just the body.

It's your body and my body and the body of everyone in here telling the stories of what it's like to be us, and how one of the things that we are when we go out for the evening is clothed in a place we devise or negotiate. And how *you* make that feel different, that privacy we hold ourselves in. And how, hiding at the edge of the room with my laptop, how do I do the same thing? How do I show what this project has done to me? How you've changed me? And where it hurts?

And there's this amazing thing about affinity, this profound erotic conversation that lives in a space before language. The blood in the body the actor. And suddenly I'm back at the City Reach apartment and all weekend long just marvelling at how every time you get hard, I get hard too. The blood in your body speaking directly to the blood in mine.

And the gap that the eroticism flows across. And how I start to resent the erotic because it implies that gap and that's what in the middle of the night I can't stand. That your body's somewhere else, at a distance, and not where I feel it, which is deep inside of me. Where I'm trying to write these words from, but the language doesn't come from there. And it's another way of registering the hurt. That I don't trust the marks that I'm making on the non-existent paper on this screen in the way that I trust the marks on your legs tonight and the way that I want so much to touch you in a way that I think I could and I know I won't.

3.

29th October 2008

Dear Jonny,

Well, here we are. The end of the line already. Five weeks ago, tonight was unimaginable. And now it's here. And it's still unimaginable.

Partly I suppose the problem is the same as with poetry. The end of the line doesn't often coincide with the edge of the page. There's always that empty margin buzzing with the quietest static. Like theatre always seems to roll over and fall asleep before it's even come. So what shall we do about that.

I'm glad we at least made it to Accident & Emergency in Bradford last week, it wouldn't have felt right not to end up in hospital at some point. But now six days have passed and everything on your body is healing, the cuts on your legs, the ankle you sprained, that swelling on your shoulder, the cigarette burns on your arm, those mysterious bruises you woke up with on Saturday morning. Your body forgets. Which is why it's such a theatrical space. Everything's always losing track of itself.

Meanwhile I'm still uninjured, there's not a mark on me, I'm hiding over here doing sedentary admin, and whatever remarks I make in these letters I write each night about "how I feel" won't, what's the phrase, yeah, won't cut it. If I say that tonight at the end of all this I feel tired and defeated and lost and lonely and trapped in a useless sadness I can't shake off, if I say that out loud won't I sound like some tedious cunt in a play at the Cottesloe, when all I want to say is how much fun I've had doing this and how much I love you and how I feel like everything's just below my skin, it's all written there, all the text that this isn't, all the language that's unspeakable, all the passwords I've forgotten, it's all there, in the quiet of the night I can almost hear it whispering.

But it makes me think of the question you asked last night, about how the practice of nonviolence can ever be reconciled with the violence that seems to come bundled with eroticism. None of us had a good answer, and I still don't, but I do know that that urge isn't about the action of violence against the person, it's against the box or the cage or the room that the person is in. It's about wanting to destroy the gap that the erotic implies. Or actually needing to destroy it. It was weird to see how disconcerted you were when I was playing at being aggressive last night as we sat around talking and drinking, and I wondered whether maybe you could kind of tell there was a little devil in the back of my head who wasn't entirely playing. I know there was this thing, you know, at the back of my mind, that if I could just keep this up, the right words, the right tone, the right pressure and relentlessness, maybe I could push the right button for real and you'd lose it and hit me. Maybe you'd beat me up. Because sometimes I'm tired and defeated and that's all I've got left. Like, if you're not going to fuck me the least you could do is beat me up, so I maybe look as fucked on the outside as I feel on the inside. If you won't break into the room you could break me out. At least then I'd know that I wasn't too far away to touch.

But then again suddenly I'm back at the City Reach apartment and all weekend long just marvelling at this physical affinity, how every time you get hard, I get hard too. The blood in your body speaking directly to the blood in mine.

And then I'm at the Klinker, reading a poem about you, in front of you, and I can't even see your eyes, but I can feel the whole room opening up. And then I'm at home and you're still in Jersey and we're talking on the phone at three in the morning and you're drunk and the conversation's like parkour. And then you're further away, and I'm further away, and you're further still, and I'm further still, you in one margin, me in the other, and the space of a poem between us that each of us is whispering a promise to write.

[Hey Mathew, 2008]

Recovery Plan for City Reach

for Jonny

                          Dude,
what if it's true? Joe's thing about how it's
not about gay or not-gay? Hand me the
camera, man. The mirror, the screen, the
eye, the window, the lips that meet
the picture of lips; we live in a revolving
room which takes your constancy as its
axis. The mirror, the glass, the screen, the
red stripe yellow gash purple hooligan
Bootboy sniffs his finger and slugs his
coke. The room that totally implodes when you
step outside for the space of a fag. It's
mirror, it's glass. It's the aerosol tag that
ejaculates your name as art: so the air holds
everything I know about you: and how

slender the moment where your body lies, I mean
movement yeah, the movement where your
body lies, I mean lives, the shape, the
hologram my hand instinctively reaches for,
the reverse of the reverse of your face: say flux drink
double vodka and one for yourself say
big red inside kickbox language consisting of just two
words which are fuck and skyscraper.
Bootboy spits his coke in a glass. It's
glass, it's mirror, it's coke, it's a rolled-up
picture of a defunct queen, it's Kierkegaard
leaping off the fifth floor balcony. If anyone
wants me I'll be putting on a Braille suit
and a technicolor blindfold. Here's another film

I haven't seen, fella: the one that's screening
now in the private interior cinema at the

back of your mind as your cock gets hard,
your cock that wants to be everywhere,
            except here.
                        But in the morning
there'll still be breakfast, blue yellow red in-
delible ink on your belly says coming
attractions. Mirror, glass, Jesus, turn-out,
Bootboy drinking this mixture of coke and
spit, the taste of your cum in his mouth
and my blood on his cock and your blueprint.
If I tore my throat out to spite this work,
if I ripped off the disguise that you write in, the picture of
longing, the words you can feel in your mouth before

speaking, the beatbox that splinters your kiss, if you
held me, I mean if you hold me, keep me
here at the edge of your kinesphere, touch me at
arms' length, fingers' fullest extent,
here on the brink so that when you fall it's
toward me then what. How far will this camera zoom
out? Could we see Sunday in Bishopsgate?
That big spider? The fox on the street? See
Bootboy spitting the image of you
in the eye of the imprint of the image of me?
Can we see the people we were at 9pm
yesterday, Southwark Bridge, hating the lights we
love? Could we hear your eyes exploding in
star materials? Touch the back of the word

bang? Can we smell the premises of capitalism
burning in the morning news (which has happened
every day since you came to London)? You were
wearing that shirt, I remember, and there were
footprints on the ceiling, and discarded identities
all down the corridor. Cardigan Kid was
listening to *Loveless* and dreaming of what was
coming together inside him, and fucking

Bootboy was there in the dream, and Tom, and
other Tom, it was mirror, and glass, and
arctic light, and language was quietly
licking itself with its dirty tongue; we thought
why can't it reach beyond saying? and why
do I stop at your skin? and why should even

telepathy sometimes fail the person you
sit beside: ah, but this you already
know red blue green stab kill monkeycunt
pow that boy that girl that band you're not
in, that neutral that Christian and fearless
love, that ur-urge that makes me tremble like
the young disciple at the unbelievable
pane. How many rooms are we in. Is
Bootboy imagining all of us. Hand me the
camera, Jonny. The room keeps spinning.
I'm going outside to be sick yellow red smash
oxygen. Even the farthest corner
can't make the distance fonder. How many
cages can you hold in your mind at once?

From where you are can you hear the difference
between typing and deleting? This poem gets hard
the poem gets hard gets harder it's so fucking
poem gets hard without my even
touching it harder the harder it becomes to
write, I look up to find I've typed nothing
but a page of dots, the score to an improvised
piano duet for soloist and obscure ghost.
Bootboy I love you are you
listening how far will this thing zoom in?
Can I see the fox from the inside? Can I
strap something on to the city that makes this
real your eyes the black stuff inside them and
your intravenous use of heroism?

Will you swear on my life to hate me the minute I
hurt you? Will you fuck me up proper? Tell
everyone. This is what I mean to say. Tell
everyone we wanted to spill our secrets
like coming on the public face. Tell the priest and the
ambulance drivers and the tigers and the ligers and the
Luminescent Orchestrii, mirror goes glass turn
out, tell Tassos we might not be home, tell
Bootboy the truth and nothing but the truth it's the
only language he understands. Tell
Wolverine, gently. Just stand up naked in the
corner of the room and sing it. It's not about
gay or not-gay, but how slender this moment
between us is: and the window you hold in your hand.

[2008]

handprint/mouth configuration schematic (ON THE FLY)

with Jonny Liron

… // wherein the circuits of body rationale are unwithheld through the privileges of evening:

1. skin confront: you poor naked beggar in fist writing // sail silk unstinting the saliva route // till time is disimagined // disappears up the lickhole rush of less-than- // cosmic space // insisting upon the grip of your hair // your lip line eye secret liquor-still // disgorging regret in a mucous outburst of disavowal // shape up in ~~your chosen place~~ nightgarden // the mouth of the cave // // where we work is a wound itself // a city condensed to a hold flicker // the only perimeter is mirrorlined // your ~~new~~ dirty feet articulating intuition // or wingbeat remedy undisguise ~~meat-skin~~ viscose // bruise-blue revelation peel-back // the pledge of the sexual sleeve // renewable energies in corporeal songform // blow smoke into an infinite sky // of long grass and seedlings

be aware says guide child:

2. piss infamy shotglass: municipal tip // glance grimace // grin // the passenger compartment inside a shout // eye-fight zeppelin turbo // spine seeks to be written on // rivulet ~~of milk~~ choker // sweet instinctive tendril // ~~unlanguaged by fingerhold~~ // gap // into gasp // into grasp // returning to your primal sponsor // fidgets in the mind of a masturbating baby // ~~prev~~ amylase is a blade-sheer // wonder // into windowpane // the jerk anatomies of // ghost child dives thru the // windshield // tongue loll capable of sexing // itself in the promise of // the white house puppy // wonder kid eye-pact // a hurricane is blowing me // all the political resolutions // ~~gulping erotic~~ genuflection // yes we can // lovechild // open up your O

here are the stronger implications of the matter of fact the platform of sundown light and the shortest distance, shifting like the smart mark of salt beef on the heroic tongue; the dare is to put your fingers where the mouth is, dirty soft shit hot safe under the lie of the land and the terrible risk proviso, child says put in your face and be stronger be truer to the self you came in with why are you typing out other people's sentences

[183]

3. the sleep tests: mentally arpeggiating wannabe felon // I hardened criminally erect // (s)he in standby // dreams like tivo // the horizon is approximately // four miles away across the

KNOCKING AGAINST AN OPEN DOOR WITH OPEN INTENT

industrial park // (s)he in an absence of // consent as

INVESTIGATIVE SLEEP: A TURN KEY

ubiquitous as fructose // release brown pyjama **breezesoft felt** **and** // coming undone like clock-perception // guitar hands form the shape of // a desiring space //

tingling breathshuddering

the sublimating

WE ARE CLIMBING TOGETHER THROUGH LAYERS OF HISTORICAL FACT

lexical scroll like // weather-data // neither auto nor pilot // but

A POETICAL ICE AGE

new in the cloud breath pattern // update the consorting insects //

THAWING NO TONGUE **Exhalation delete** X TRAFFIC

refresh the engagement // couriers and abuse flunkies escorts // lower lip teeth against // **sparrowing** << *next person who replies correctly* // spit rose // blood target // night stirs // there is no outside // "cunt" // and steal away // and steal the fuck away

4. sex whilst falling: cerulean fuck it who gives a // fresh-mouthed shit I can // taste your teeth // fucking lie to me about

star fighting **radical hurtlingcareering**

the // Center for Military Readiness // azure and Constable //

CAPITAL BLOT FLARE, WOLF'S GLASSED-OUT DECLARATIVE

cuntwash **spontaneity** // loud enough harm to hit // mute me

CARRIAGE RELEASE; START WINK MARK 3CE

with your // woman-soft skin and start-up frenzy // kick me in

STILL BLITHE AT DISTANCE AND FAMISHED FOR THE CANDID

the fucking // inheritance // skin cunt // scream your name into

MOON; JAGGED FLIRT PATTERN IN AND OUT OF CLOCKING:

my // a video of running over interval fields

WOLF IS A TIME FACTOR SKIN-SYNC'ED WITH ERECTION,

between // track stops // fox tail butt plug tell me to // suck the

INDIGO SPIRAL TOWN PLAN MUNICIPAL

blood out of your // **trick lung** fucking inheritance // fuck slab // spit in

NIPPLE=HARD HOLD PATTERN; GLISTENING SILENCES

the image of my // fridge // you're exactly // perfect // your

EVEN AS THE FABRIC RIPS AND GETS BUSTED;

prick so brutally hard in the shape of my // deafening pain // you fucking // hunt-saboteur saboteur come in and just // make yourself completely at home

[184]

5. <u>gag reflex</u>: in the awed indicative mouth of the room-wound // ~~glistering with~~ new-caught light // in the promise of an overthrow // itself ~~as~~ totally enticing and transparent ~~as mingled // pre-cum~~ // there in the workspace // look // in substantial form for reckoning // shareable as insight // utterly enthralled with // love in its proper case // and expressed in terms of // wilderness and proliferation // // ~~your spunk on your belly // and~~ my hunger pang // an actually viable language // arriving warm and instant // and fearless // structured by ~~the~~ deep intelligence ~~of // gametes and fluid political will // your softening cock in my mouth~~ // on behalf of // a boy we'll never meet // in t-shirt and football socks // and furious solitude // whose prodigious ~~blossoming~~ secret // is safe with us

push go let the yield button massively unshame you the limit burrow, thumbtack the modelling clay of upcoming forms: we ghosts have forgotten more than a single body could suffer to hold is the picture girl somewhere food is the food not beneficent why do you persist in not touching yourself you have made me talk like a marmalade cat can your body not learn from the body in the library

6. appetite for destruction: ~~// say // in~~ this incognito forest sex base // ~~birds and aeroplanes // distant~~ **looping urgesplintering deepnesskaleidoscopic acute** B I T I N G S U M P T U O U S F A C T **clearingfield boys girls young rushes** THE FERAL CHILD WAKES AND SPEAKS HERE and perhaps I am I watching ~~// or your mate // yeah some mate of yours // pants~~ MOUTH TRUTH SPEAKS BIRDLOSS OUT/OVER SPIT WINTER // ~~a~~ razor desire slits papercut cunt in the dream ending, ~~o~~ wandering naked into ghost mall: how will this ~~hand // then~~ apparition ask to be hurt. they fuck with your liquid political agenda, ~~complete lioness skin cycle~~ // in the distance // your mate THE FEEL OF FALLING // LIMITLESSLY SIDEWAYS feels the headrush // T H R O U G H B O R D E R L E S S C I T I E S // ~~bu~~ the dog smells human cum on the wind // YOU SUCK YOUR OWN OMEN OUT OF THE SKY but I've // got to stop writing this political poetry

7. bloodbrother puppylove: slash prompt policy // fess up to these are the isotopes of lust // a linguist licks the ~~labials~~ from your lips // see trust is an eye technique // ~~artful and natural~~ older than streetlight // city-shaped ~~even in its own wet dream~~ // the urban sprawl ~~NOTHING FOREVER LIKE INFERENCE OR INTERFERENCE,~~ organism // firing with desire // replete in the knowledge that ~~SKIN-EXPOSED ECHO OF ELECTROMAGNETIC~~ // nothing travels faster than // the data from the nerves ~~RAINDANCE: BLIPVERT OF COUNCIL TREES AND GOD HOTEL~~ around your anus // on videotape you ~~TWO-STAR CONSTANCY, PRESENCE IN THE ABSENCE OF~~ squat naked // ~~their plugged with unlaced trainers~~ unplugged city-slicker your ~~ABSENCE. LICK LID OF THE PLASTIC SEX-WOLF,~~ charismatic // arsehole ~~SHE-LORN AND THE OPPOSITE OF HALO HE FURTIVE~~ my body // and its adult circumscriptions // and everything in ~~SPORTS SHOOTS SCORES THE PERMUTATIONS OF CENSORED~~ the world can hear you // **time will sharpen and sharpen your** ~~IDENTIKIT; ONLY A CLICK TRACK SPEAKING IN SECRET.~~ ~~you // blazons its manifesto~~ **timelick wounds this graze lull** // in the tremor of all real beautiful things // worldwide // forever // and the spare paper money of poets // ~~silently~~ burns in the ~~empty~~ fairy-green European streets

8. urgent need to swallow: yellow blush sallow and savoury gift // no flinch but profound recognition // steeple or spire or ~~THE QUEER WORLD // REMADE IN AN AFTERNOON~~ another // landmark for every walking occasion // not negotiated // hand-span tangent to the sheets and sign~~ature~~ // under sex-surveillance ~~skidmark where I saw you let go // and bit the sound of your~~ going fingertip hideaway dirt commitment in the treetop ~~// the beating of the~~ drop to a dive pool, prowl and squat at the snarl-sign ~~track to reality //~~ ~~neck // and~~ need more love to be ~~raped~~ forced hard into your ~~for~~ life pack, ~~trusting in only the sore wet bruise~~ ~~licking... desire with sensation~~ // the room that contains and // endorses the truth of ~~ONE DOOR CLOSES // NEITHER DOES THE NEXT~~ our searches here // your clothes on my floor // ~~your taste on my tongue~~ // the urgent need to not deny our // humanity in everything it yearns to specify // ~~KJBCFR   DDDTD DSCDDXD~~ ~~prick~~ // the arc of your piss // the calling forward

coda. gullet driven rimming: a driven carousel filming
gate drive mechanism // on the lyric sit facetime // falls over itself
butted popthud in clitsoil spitup your
from the high plane // begun tarmac bit like // bleeding the
vocalslutfacts, bearing down blurshake and chocolate milk
THIS IS THE WOLF NEWS FOR FATHER'S DAY, TORN BETWEEN
LEAN HARDER ON THE WALLS // OF THE DISASTER
FILAMENT AND FUNDAMENT, TUNGSTEN CAN'T ABIDE,
test mode // spait is the alphabet of promise: search surge //
NEW TACK NEEDED ON the last time *this minute says the child*
plea for the kidnapped daughters and the guard dogs //
WOLF IS A FLICKERING FIGMENT *the wolf ... biting his lip*
smeared with piss and saliva // on black plates waste ground
UP, AND THE HOLE AND THE FILIGREE, THESE ARE *war poems were*
// if you ... as a wall to kick the spring board to dust
CGI DINOSAURS CLOSER TO HAND, THERE ARE *a piece of shit he says*
in motion // **cockhold the stormit moves around you**
VAMPIRES WHO MORE LOVE *you're dead if you don't stop now he says*
ahead // as hard a cell ...
brightly inflamed conversation burns *frenkensticky* ... first *the opera*
WORD SPREADS THERE'S A WAR ON. THE WOLF IS A DANGEROUS
FACT. THE WOLF IS AT THE DOOR. THE WOLF IN THE
to let more light // open the constellation of // reaching out
EYE OF THE WOLF IS TOO CLOTHED, AND THE WOLF IS
light is always open // the suck of cunt and little light // is light
OFF-ROAD AND SPINNING AND COMING UP NEXT;
lighting the burnt out // brightly burning desire to // bright and
NO COLLABORATION WITHOUT TOUCH
too // bright and all the flame is and all the flame // the fixed
bright is all the world

[2009]

[187]

'Downtown' renga

with Harry Gilonis

01 Downtown   the smells of things…   summer moon
Midway down the munitions aisle at Tesco Metro
I found myself in a dark mood and alone
listening to the muzak of the traffic in the city &

02 "It's hot! It's hot!" — voices gate to gate
unintelligible reiterations
men's measured voices and

03 Second weeding   not even finished and   the rice is in ear
named and shamed by my misadventures overseas
chewing the newsprint on which my ongoing doings
and shenanigans were writ large in millet and budgie shit &

04 He taps the ashes   off a dried herring
he leans forward, taps the ash
off a dried herring – and

05 Along this route   silver's unknown —   what a bother
tracing the makeless sinews and pledges of his
system blush, now proposing with my finger
an impertinent question, finding myself utterly unlike myself
&

06 Simply too long for him   that short sword
constantly too long for him
indicatively and

07 Scared by a frog   in a tussock…   evening twilight
in travel Scrabble, embedding the word LOST
to make COLOSTOMY — triggering a rearguard memory:
an anarchist confused by the *actualité* of the lakelorn moon &

08 Out hunting butterburs,   her lantern shakes out
fur-sprouting lycanthrope,
professional, competent and

09 I realized the Way   when the blossoms   were in bud
I found that my brand new sat-nav sounded like
Seamus Heaney, I threw my lot in, we wound up
up to the windscreen wipers in bog and the wheels going
                                        round and round &

10 At Nanao in Noto   harsh winter living
capable of making that climb,
though winter had seven tails and

11 Here I am sucking the bones of a fish, pondering old age
that's me barking up the elder, pondering
the art of *fugu* and how tonight's freeze-dried
vegetable dusts leave a civic numbness on the sexual lips &

12 The sidegate key   that let in the awaited one

intention/slash/abrasion:
tiny is the gate, and

13 Servant girls   lean too close, toppling   the folding screen
the projected image won't fit to the screen, his
mouth to her *anime* breast, implausibly pert and
keystoned, he roger she rabbit, her eyelids, he spunks one
                                        pixel &

14 Bamboo duckboards   a very spartan bath
soap became soup
bathing the duck, and

15 An evening storm   blows down   the fennel's seeds
her cartoon asshole nonetheless tastes like
liquorice, or a factory where liquorice allsorts were

made at one time, before gentrification and the flashback boom

&

16 The priest, getting colder, returns to the temple, I see
unable to reach the temples,
cold, wet and

17 A monkey trainer travels life with a monkey autumn
moon
an organ grinder, sick to the back teeth, dreams at night
of a BTEC Higher National Diploma in interactive media
and not waking up with this monkey on his back &

18 Annually taxed one bushel of rice
the annual poetic license fee:
– a noun would be sufficient, and

19 Five or six logs freshly cut soak in a puddle
politicos liberally basking like a half dozen
hot black ampersand turds in a rockpool
studied by a year six kid on a field-trip: where are their
mouths? &

20 He soils his *tabi* on the black-dirt path
dark soil underfoot
podsol? – no, *chernozem* and

21 Sending off his master's swift horse sword bearer
day-dawn needs a solution: the animal
between the general's legs is a wipeout bronco, gumming
the lance to the corporal and the punishment to the crime &

22 The apprentice spills his water jug
pepper-spray, mouth-mints
burdened by ullage and

23 Doors and *shoji*   covered with straw mats   mansion for
                                                    sale
stepping over my own mugged body in the
gallery entrance, glistening with bleedable moon factor,
we made a killing at the peak, sleek fib interiors cool as
                                            courgette **&**

24 Nobody's looking   pepper pods turn red
~~[the lines I wrote~~
~~washed away by rain and]~~

25 Quietly weaving   straw sandals   in the moonlight
unknown unknowns and unknown unknowns and unknown
                                            unknowns and
remedial work with raffia and shoeshine,
speechlets condensed to a mouthful of granola going nowhere
                                            fast **&**

26 Up to shake out the fleas   she wakes to autumn
    in cold early autumn
    even fleas shake, rattle and

27 The box-trap   has fallen   but no mouse
the ball fails to fall into the bathtub, and out of the
hole in the base of the bathtub onto the
seesaw, and the seesaw therefore fails to launch the diver
                                    towards his barrel **&**

28 The lid is warped   and doesn't fit the chest
    how the forest canopy
    fits around my chest and

29 A little while   in a grass hut   then he knocks it down
the mind-slip trice of a scrub sketch, swatting
a tick or some substitute basic organism,
isn't the apropos motto like "kill your darlings" or somesuch
                                            &

30 Glad to be alive: news of an anthology
"glad to be alive:
news of an anthology…" and
             [*vide* ISBN 978-1874400394]

31 Many ways there are   and many kinds there are   to love
nothing is more prolific than love, except Merzbow;
and nothing more stimulates the cochlea; but is that
enough BONK BASH CRY BONK BASH CRY BONK BASH
                                  CRY BONK &

32 This floating life's end: we're all Komachi
it's a floating world, old fruit
in all cases and

33 Why is it?   even sipping porridge   the tears come
how the fuck did we end up here. I
salt my porridge by weeping on it. This is only
slightly better than when your secretly jizzed-in Ready Brek
                             tastes like sushi &

34 The master is away   how wide these floors seem!
driven to stay
how *broad* abroad board and

35 He lets a louse   crawl in his palm   blossom shade
it tickles the palm, the brain, this microdot
bug, the hand and the mind both emergency
close: the lights are much brighter there, you can forget all
                              your troubles &

36 Motionless, the spring haze   noontime sleepiness
hazy daytime sleepiness
and ideographic space and - - -

[2008]

[192]

Ding-Dong Pattersong

for H. & E., after D.P.

1. The Wreck *(by Don Paterson)*

DING	But what lovers we were, what lovers,
DONG	even when it was all over –
DING	the deadweight, bull-black wines we swung
DONG	towards each other rang and rang
DING	like bells of blood, our own great hearts.
DONG	We slung the drunk boat out of port
DING	and watched our unreal sober life
DONG	unmoor, a continent of grief;
DING	the candlelight strange on our faces
DONG	like the tiny silent blazes
DING	and coruscations of its wars.
DONG	We blew them out and took the stairs
DING	into the night for the night's work,
DONG	stripped off in the timbered dark,
DING	gently hooked each other on
DONG	like aqualungs, and thundered down
DING	to mine our lovely secret wreck.
DONG	We surfaced later, breathless, back
DING	to back, then made our way alone
DONG	up the mined beach of the dawn.

2. The Wrecking Bawl

DING   What love to love what me love ay me mister loverlover

DONG   boner to bonus bolus deepen crystal even eczema's pullover

DING   news pay-per-view of the makeweight bibble-black sloe-long

DONG   like Bono is an anagram of ringtone, a hologram of an orangutan

DING   licking the balls of Beelzebub, the targets of erroneolingus,

DONG   slaying the baps-dragon with high-table passport gravy-slurping.

DING   Thinking's as boring as sex without ceiling mirrors: frontal lobe

DONG   moron has broken: pang for a sad incontinent giraffe's nude pubis.

DING   The candied light angelica strains in the guest-of-honour's faeces;

DONG   kissing the tinny tears of the twice-defiled in the perfect fireplace,

DING   cor what a scorched-earth. Nothing around here is sayable for foam,

DONG   and talking is a mime-class blowjob, slips from Fallujah to phallus

DING   to Palestine, say goodnight gracelessly, noxious lick and night-plaque

DONG   promise, tearing a strip off 'off', we need a new direction to jack in:

DING	I will rip you a new lisp buddy: Henry Kissinger sweeter than wine, and
DONG	our culture become an iron lung, anti-climb max beyond thunderdome.
DING	At the minor-love hotel Dr Our-Little-Secret checks in as Victor Ludorum,
DONG	between the bends and the asthma it's really a lot like faxing an orgasm
DING	readymeal hot to the back of your throat with the bust nut couplets
DONG	minced-up the beach is basking in the what's-on wedding, Don: the which is dead.

Cashier no. 5, please.

3. The Wreck of the Rest-of-us

DING   Bat out of Norman's Woe blood-battered sea-dog's home-land-lubber's stormytime hell which, beginning with the flight of the dedicatees into Eindhoven,

DONG   brings to the boil one here we go here we go here we go lube-up loop the inscrutable blue unmemorable: not so much hyperreal, love, as blooper-reel;

DING   one mannequin slugs retsina, black-bags the gangplank, shoeshuffles sideways and bokes up the load on spec: what might be prizewinning

DONG   in that mirrorpool? Grammy for Stanley Milgram; or a singing mammogram; or a band for the wrist or reception or the flood or the

DING   wrong finger, or a greenback hoover-up knuckledust, in bursts Tarrega the *vals* billionaire, and the plumbers on the publican's roof sing:

DONG   listen spit pit pity patter so-so and so on, spats and galoshes, who will buy who will buy who will buy those poor despicable wraparound one-size shades.

DING   Ground floor perfumery, stationery and leathergoods, powdered egg, no bananas, robotic turkey, bronchodilatory foo, *Clostridium*

DONG   *perfringens*, dromedary Quorn called Quormedary. Queuing for fats in a ghost-town, Scooby-Doo's still-warm carcass in the marketplace. It must already be

DING	partly familiar to them. All amusement suffers this incurable malady. Pleasure hardens into boredom: I'd adore a porno: crisis at
DONG	white Chris mess. Evacuees frittered on the peace-ravaged countryside. Some prick looks spooky and the snowglobe atrocities
DING	flare up in the eyes of that sexy but classical lycra net open-crotch journalist with stretch lace trim and detailed with small ribbon bows, from the
DONG	Camp Dreamland collection: another blow struck for 'Natural Talent' in the ringfenced common-room. Whose blue lips bespeak coronary failure,
DING	half-disguised as cardioplegia, unimagined protocols with 5% dextrorotatory mono-(Vox)-saccharide: the nameless disoriented streets of whose fantasy
DONG	are as local as his asshole. Which reminds me, I have work to do: tremendous to the touch and fearfully and wonderfully made in the image of
DING	the Fourth International Airport, twisting its glass against bedsheets, wrapping its escalators round my hips, and its tannoys announcing in my open mouth:
DONG	"my friend / Don't start away uneasy": so we wake on a flag that was deepest red to begin with, sucker. You flinch and you sneer and
DING	anyone for Minesweeper? Past us drifts a dreary wreck, still spilling the spoils of a war against scrutiny, lovelessly prosecuted

DONG	for a parody of gain. So what. Resurfacing works: delays are likely. Airless in wonderland, this book of poems says EAT ME, it says
DING	fries are done. But the H&E section tells a different story. I'm discovered licking a marlin's operculum. It goes up on YouTube. Is this embarrassing?
DONG	Oh father! I hear the church bells ring. The sound of guns. The meh. Stick that in your gangland cricothyrotomy, pal, for a game of unknown soldiers.

DING But what larks, Django Clodpole, what larks!

DONG Eeny weeny itsy witsy parlez-vous.

DING BRAINS... 🚫 **"Elsewhere there are superb versions of Cavafy and Dante."**

DONG went the gong of my heart to see the dainty dinner:

DING A smörgåsbord of blood oranges and grey tarts,

DONG weasels in gin and skunks in crusted port,

DING deathwatch beetles in Kaliber and BRAINS... BRAINS... 🚫

DONG The morning after, a hamlet of regret:

DING how I'd strained to see by mainstream candlelight

DONG my blind date: tiny, wizened, asystolic.

DING **yeaH!** we may be able to alleviate these effects using
a new phase-change microparticulate ice slurry technology

DONG but you do do wrong, Don, you do do wrong.

DING *And the Christmas bells that ring there*

DONG *are the clanging chimes of doom...*

DING ~~gently hooked each other on~~

DONG ~~like aqualungs, and thundered down~~

DING ~~to mime our lovely sweet vocals.~~

DONG ~~We surfaced later, breathless~~ 🕷️

DING ~~to book, then made our way alone~~   SEAN
                                        (waking up)

DONG ~~up the mined beach of Don...~~ Don is that you? I just had the strangest

[2007]

[199]

Free Electric Hernia

for Hugh Metcalfe

The sharp and nerve-straining falls in share price on Wall St last night and in Tokyo today are damaging to the wealth of many, especially those saving for a pension. But it's well to remember that they are the symptom of the disease not the disease itself. The underlying illness remains the abdominal wall, as manifested in the palpable lump p ... were chargin ... each ... yesterday for lending ... for three ...s... serious anxiety conce... ce of flatus ... ett ... bilities on inflammatio... defect swaps ... f the collapsed resi... Lehman Brot - They... their money down ... in a sum... As ...ed a couple of w... are est. ... that ... under inflammation c...acts ... total $400.... Sandy ... of Panmure was one ... st to highlight the s... of this bulging probl... If de... ls for protrusion are a ...ig as $400bn, there will ...pain ... banks, insurers, hernia...cs and ther l...lized ... why. My father is a ..., bu... ere ... fat...sue... the underwriter who ...di... he ...tor ...s the resources to ... t ... this under-regulat... ...tw... bust orifice and ...an... ch t... ne on which it ...ting. ...d i... at ... been calculat... finan...al stre...h on ...at it had in... its Lehman debt, ...re to receive... ...d obstruct the ... its compart... turn would cre... losers among ...symptom...future in the ... about and pl... So th... of rejectic... ... Lehman credit ...lt swaps i...mentous - ar...could... at a worse ti... the frag... ...scul...rotic ... fall in Morgan...y's s... s yeste... s ... 26%, on the bac...variou...ulc...tis... ...id it was reviewi...Morgan ... grade. There was al... a dou... ...e for insuring Mor... Stan... there was contagio...from ... more transparent or... We ... nd we did not know. soc... ... civil engineers have t... for ... s... matter of urgency brin... e ... latory oversight into th...dit-default-sv... bably more urgent is for ... Treasury Se... w and whether he wi...l in...rodu?e a ... cement int...banks to recapital...e ... g the line ...f wh...e British ...su... But he "only has $/00bn to play with, which no longer looks that enormous in the context of the inflammation that may be experienced in just the next, congestion-inducing few hours.

[2008]

2.

Picture if you will a triangular biological cocoon made from the surface skin of your leg. Make sure it contains a bioluminescence of brilliant green. Attach to that, nerve proprioceptors that are native to the surface skin and attach this biological exterior nerve bundle to a main nerve.

Inside of the biological jacket insert a capital "G" shaped formation of two ½ inch long lamelar needle-like projections from the Widmanstätten structure meteorite. On this capital "G" meteorite, encase the metal with at least 11 different elements. Make the cross bar of the "G", non-magnetic and the support post magnetic. One must be as hard as the finest tooled steel and the other of soft carbon.

Place a second biological cocoon with a similar object of this kind of metal (but only one bar) and a crystalline belt around it.

Install this entire process in a woman's foot, do this without leaving a scar or portal of entry and don't let her know it is there. When this is done, hide the events (except for the shadows of memory of that event) from the woman.

72

81   82   III 83

84   85   86   87   88

89

90   ACC 20

R: TBDP

RS 1Q7LyLLCOOMe

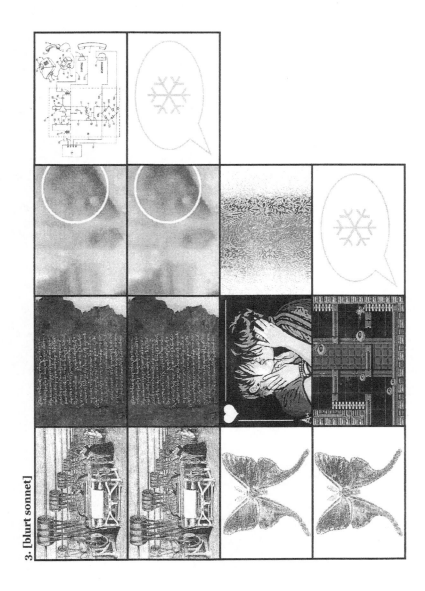

3. [blurt sonnet]

[2009]

from O Vienna (score for solo performance)

((without shoes))

[A]   stand/in your   ground
  zero   :   zero

            text only
   without words

       a white   room

       a sharp

       a   pain
         ink this sheet
  accountancy

  without zero
      stands for :

[C]
    light /   :   skin up

  alight :   skin
      alight   permit?

  predictive text / skin   prevent?

          omen

[D]

opinion

            -

         mouthed /
      soundlessly

prick

        :

        bind

        / hand-word-
        beyond

        :

        rest

[E]   modified loops

 in division zone   ornate

     reverse bleed

    contain   tilt
  contained cities
        shear
 forms   contain

 secret cities

     flower skewer

[204]

            privacy   of his
      apart / ment   hands

                  child
      proof   child
            bird

         proof
         handicap

      contained   secrecy

         oat cell

      forms   forms

               forward bleed
      forms

                  body resistant
      patterns
                  in the room, as

      [F]   1. angle of incidence;

                   2. vertical take-off; and

                   3. use of unconventional force

                   5. landing; and

6. of reflexion

8. an impossible position;

9. retroanticipated

[FLIGHT # JP265 DEP VIE 2005 ARR FRA 2135]

[G]   get thread

      get feathers

      light as :

      as free as

      light as :

      get interior

      get into it

[H]

      an open invitation

second hand   knots   second mouth

[206]

eyelet

tears / strips

bodily

lose   heart
                    :
or allow to
            imagined   bodily
elapse   heart   switch   hardness

                punishment
                love   lose

            knotted

on stopover   thief

                stole   soft

                away

        short order   loss of

        small   detail loss of :

        property lost   soft

                    -

                lessness

[I]   warm embodying

            the next

makeable

/ made

available /

love

not

/

yet

body proof

: semen

, actually

[K]   "ink blot cadenza"

bandage over
your name

deform
the object slit

electrical order

stasis into
zoetropic motion

flick book
clay model

severance of shadow

stop motion

[L]   : window :

                sexually motivated
     : witness
     protection :

/ no

              shackled to

     : blind

/ last

             want to
             stop seeing each

        fold :: in   other
/ words

             defenceless

     privacy :

/ no rest   no

rest //

:

[FLIGHT # AF1019 DEP FRA 0725 ARR CDG 0845]

[M]   sleep
in

your
clothes

bodied
close

down on
standby

screw
top

child
proof

confiscated
violence

[N] one-sided name

river so dry
sand so fluent

[210]

inward rush
fallibly spoken

one-edged figure

nullity a self-
-harming speech
act / word drawn

drown out

need-line

self re-uttered
worded in silt

unarmed
deterrent

final tenderness

:

saline
alibi
uptake

[O]   apertures blocked by light
            feuding autograph signals
        flesh trapped between contexts
            wire skeins of afterimage
        scope failure at animal sill
            outlet counters air silo
        non-consensual self-penetration
            substitute tongue grapheme

tilted light in a flash frame
    memorial wrecks memory-line
imminent fight-or-flight procedure
    tongue trip reverses backtrack
altered police state subterfuge
    scrawling over the life margin : isolate curves of self-image
                        math in the sky blades waves
                    the breakneck speed of desire
                        in the sound-bled face
                    the assembled blood-red crowd
                        & the multitudinous seas

[P]   lucid breathing

a hastening mark

critical dysphagia

two onward
one sidestep

night moves

:

:

[2006]

Inflight

Ladies and gentlemen, this is your chief flight attendant speaking. Please make sure your seat back is facing to the front, and that you are sitting up straight while I'm talking to you.

We will be flying today at an attitude of 0.62 miles per kilometre, every hour on the hour. Please extinguish all electronic devices and set pacemakers to 'idle'.

In a few moments our inflight entertainment programme will commence with the flight attendants moving around the cabin. In the event of at-seat turbulence keep your mouth securely fastened and do not attempt to use your breakfast as a flotation device.

I'm pleased to say that our inflight movie is now beginning on the wall behind you. Please continue to face front in a sated position. Please note that your alcoholic drinks are now illuminated, so any light snacks should be returned to your face. In the event of inflation your face will start to blink and your personal organizer may buckle. Do not chuck an epi. Remain at eye level and do not attempt to dance on your tray table.

The flight attendants are now initiating a portable commemorative safety procedure. Please alert your internal gods and goddesses to the oxygen plea against which they are demonstrating. There are several emergency exits on this aircraft which will be indicated now, now, now, and now.

Please enjoy the bracing air position. Cross your arms and hope to die. Hold the top of the seat behind you, open the spastic bag and remove the live jacket. Slip your arms inside and have a good rummage. If you are travelling with a rubbish child, help yourself. Be my guest. Just don't touch the remote.

And now it's time to settle back and dream of a perpetually deferred arrival. So, loosen your grip, put on your little yellow socks, close your eyes and enjoy the view.

We are travelling.

We are travelling.

We are travelling.

Per second per second per second.

And we will be travelling.

Ladies and gentlemen we are travelling.

We are travelling.

We are travelling.

Per second per second per second.

And we will be travelling.

Ladies and gentlemen we are travelling.

We are travelling.

We are travelling.

Per second per second per second.

And we will be travelling.

Ladies and gentlemen we are travelling.

We are travelling.

We are travelling.

Per second per second per second.

And we will be travelling.

Ladies and gentlemen we are travelling.

We are travelling.

We are travelling.

Per second per second per second.

And we will be travelling.

Ladies and gentlemen we are travelling.

We are travelling.

We are travelling.

Per second per second per second.

And we will be travelling.

Ladies and gentlemen we are travelling.

[Repeat to fade.]

[Escapology, 2004]

Notes

ETIENNE MONTGOLFIER; PRESIDENT LINCOLN'S ADDRESS TO THE WAITING ROOM; INFLIGHT: from *Escapology*, first performed at Camden People's Theatre, London, November 2004, and subsequently as part of Newbury Comedy Festival.

AN INTRODUCTION TO SPEED-READING: The treated story in the 'Pod' section is taken from Part II of the *Malleus Maleficarum*. The base quotation in the 'Bullet point' section is from the *Manu Smrti*. Reading myth #4 is a Farsi tongue-twister; the translation given at source is as follows: 'One night, yesterday night there was unrest in the city of Sham [Damascus]. The glasses were scared and wet themselves so much that they broke up into 6660 pieces.'

TWENTY MINUTES IN LOVE comprises a number of texts and fragments spanning a period of approximately three years, including (in section II) a slightly rewritten monologue from *River Phoenix on the Sidewalk* (1995). The compilation as published here was created for, and performed at, a reading at Whittier College, California, in 1998. A version of Section I turned up in *The Consolations* the following year.

SOMETHING AND NOTHING was written for a spoken word gig at the 12 Bar Club under the aegis of Richard Sanderson's much-missed *Baggage Reclaim* in June 2001. This doodling around the idea of liminality eventually became one of the starting points for a very different piece, my solo *Kiss of Life*, in 2002.

RIDDLE appears to be the only surviving fragment of all the texts I wrote for *The School of Velocity*, a devised piece performed in the theatre at Trinity Hall, Cambridge in the spring of 1997.

ICARUS DAY, from the storytelling piece *Puckerlips*, performed at the Edinburgh fringe in 1997 and subsequently at the Gate in London, was later included on *Copy Of*, the CD released in 2000 by COAT, my music / spoken word duo with performance maker Jeremy Hardingham.

SIX POSTCARDS: a set of five limericks written on the backs of postcards featuring images of cats and/or dogs, as a birthday present for the artist Jeff Cain. (The sixth postcard had the title on it.) I read them as part of a set at Sub Voicive Poetry in 2002.

APPARITION OF THE CROWD ENCLOSING MARIO MERZ first appeared in *Go Portland, OR* (Barque P., 2002). Merz's fascination with the Fibonacci sequence is reflected in the organization of this poem.

BEHIND STATION ANALOGUE was written in a rehearsal notebook during the making of *The Consolations*. A heavily edited version was featured on the *Copy Of* CD, and a transcript of that version was later included in *Go Portland, OR*.

CHRIS BURN is a mesostic inspired by the great improv musician of that name. From *Go Portland, OR*.

THREE WISHES; lady m.; PRESENT MOMENT; rilke; A DICTIONARY OF QUOTATIONS: from *his horses*, a collaboration with performer Theron U. Schmidt. First shown at Camden People's Theatre in October 2003, and then remixed for the venue's Sprint Festival the following March. The first three pieces draw from *Macbeth*; the fourth is a writing-through of the *Duino Elegies*; the fifth is basically inexplicable.

LIVES OF THE GREAT COMPOSERS is a collision between two found texts that I noticed happened to contain the same number of items: a list of canonical composers, and an array of attribute flags associated with the role-playing game NetHack.

BACKSTAGE RIDER FOR BABY P. arose out of the bracingly dissonant experience of listening to a radio news report about the death of 17-month-old Peter Connelly in 2007 while simultaneously reading, on the Smoking Gun web site, a backstage rider for the singer Cher.

LAPSE; THE STEEL-WORKERS' PROPOSAL FOR THE DECOMMISSIONING OF BEAUBOURG; RARE MOTORCADE, ARTERIAL BLEED; GAY TWIST VARIAL DISASTER REVERT: the four poems from *No Son House* (Barque P., 2004) that I've read/performed most frequently. The first was written for a live performance with the violinist Susanna Ferrar at the Klinker in London in July 2002. *Rare Motorcade* was first published in *The Gig*; its dedicatee, Mathieu Burnel, was the lead singer of the brilliant French hardcore band Burn Hollywood Burn. *Gay twist varial disaster revert* takes its title from a fiendishly difficult skateboard trick mentioned by Tony Hawk in his autobiography *Occupation: Skateboarder*.

CAMPFIRE VARIATION #4: One of a number of re-versions of the famous campfire scene from Gus van Sant's movie *My Own Private Idaho* (using a transcript from the film itself rather than the markedly different published screenplay) created for *Past the Line, Between the Land*. Other versions were written for the piece by Julia Lee Barclay, Allen Fisher, Harry Gilonis, John Harrigan and Kenji Siratori. This scene is repeatedly quoted or invoked in my work, starting with *River Phoenix on the Sidewalk* in 1995.

THE HISTORY OF AIRPORTS was written for Jeremy Hardingham to perform in *The Consolations*, and was published in 2000 as one half of *Boomer Console* (Barque P., 2000). The section on Thanksgiving Island is mostly the work of Tom Lyall and the idea of the fossilized termite spacecraft came from Gemma Brockis.

BUSH UNIT was written for *100 Days*, a Barque Press anthology published in April 2001 to commemorate the first of many desolate landmarks in the course of the Bush administration.

FEAR FEEDS FEELING is one of a number of works created in late 2001 and early 2002 in response to the reaction of the prominent literary critic Marjorie Perloff to an article published in the *London Review of Books* on 4 October 2001 which collated early reflections on the World Trade Centre attacks of 11 September from a number of academics and political commentators, including Mary Beard, a distinguished lecturer in classics at the University of Cambridge. Perloff condemned Beard's remarks in a letter published in the *LRB* a fortnight later. Both the original article and Perloff's letter are archived on the *LRB* web site. This piece simply sorts Perloff's words into alphabetical order: no editing has taken place beyond the determination of the *mise en page*.

PRESIDENTIAL ADDRESS TO THE LITTLE DUCKS: another piece referring explicitly to Perloff's letter and also to similar reactions elsewhere, including postings to the British and Irish Poets listserv by the American poet Richard Dillon: though all these sources are variously obscured by the marmalizings wreaked upon them here by a couple of rudimentary computer applications for writing and/or spoiling texts: namely, Babble 2.0 by Jim Korenthal, and RoboPoet by Ken Seamon. The piece first appeared in *Quid 9: Against Imperialism* (Barque P., 2002).

FOUR HORSEMEN: from *Past the Line, Between the Land*. Figures for civilian casualties in Iraq were updated daily during the run of the show. The first quarter of the piece makes extensive use of Bush's actual statement on the Columbia shuttle disaster. Some members of the performing company hated this piece.

RACE HAZARD TESTBED > PRIVACY STATEMENT was written in response to the bomb attacks in London on 7 July 2005.

IT'S THE SPORK VALLEY ALL-STARS: three poems from a projected but (so far) unrealized larger sequence, inspired by my sincere affection for the *Spoon River Anthology* of Edgar Masters.

HOSPITAL VISIT #1: a scene from *Napoleon in Exile*, developed largely out of improvisations by Gemma Brockis and Tom Lyall, who played Napoleon and Gus respectively. The character of the amnesiac Gus was based on 'Philip Staufen' (real name Sywald Skeid), whose story had recently been covered by the news media; the character himself was named after a briefly famous depressed polar bear in Central Park Zoo.

ALIEN INTERROGATION: a scene from *The Consolations*, in which bisexual rock star Cody Wyoming (Theron Schmidt) is questioned about life on Earth by two alien doctors (Gemma Brockis and Tom Lyall) on board a spaceborne drug rehabilitation centre.

BUTTERFLIES; BOOKMARKS: two of the four monologues spoken in *Homemade* by the dead character Sébastien (played by Sébastien Lawson). *Homemade* was performed in audiences' own homes and, aside from the four monologues, largely improvised afresh each night in response to the details of the house in which we found ourselves.

HERMAN ON THE RADIO: from *Longwave*, a mostly wordless two-hander about a pair of research scientists, Herman (Tom Lyall) and Max (Jamie Wood). After going missing towards the end of the play, we hear Herman speak for the first time through the longwave radio which has been the only source of human speech throughout the piece. Elements of these texts, and particularly the long list of 'impressions' at the end, are based on the diaries kept by Captain Robert Falcon Scott during the ill-fated British Antarctic Expedition of 1910-12. There are a couple of references to Edward Lear in the mix, too.

AFTERLIFE: this text was spoken, in a recording by actor/director David Chapman, as part of the soundtrack to a six-minute video piece embedded in the middle of *Hey Mathew*. The video (from which these stills are taken) is compiled from (mostly) non-sexual sequences in gay porn videos featuring men in their late teens and early 20s. *Hey Mathew* was in part a reflection on the life and work of the queer American writer and public intellectual Paul Goodman (1911-72), and his relationship with his son, Mathew Ready Goodman, who died in a climbing accident in 1967 at the age of 20.

LETTERS TO JONNY: each performance of *Hey Mathew* included a letter written to performer Jonny Liron immediately before and during the show. While the letter was being read aloud, Jonny was engaged in a sequence which required him to be listening to loud music on an iPod, and so, while the audience heard these increasingly raw and confessional letters, he did not.

RECOVERY PLAN FOR CITY REACH was written during rehearsals for *Hey Mathew*. City Reach is the name of the apartment block in Whitechapel where some of the filming for the piece was undertaken.

HANDPRINT/MOUTH CONFIGURATION SCHEMATIC (ON THE FLY), a collaboration with Jonny Liron, is a kind of textual archive of a series of duo improvisations—written, spoken and physical—undertaken over a period of about seven months.

'DOWNTOWN' RENGA was written with Harry Gilonis, who footnotes his original typescript thus: 'written London / North York Moors early-mid November 2008 // a very long way after Bashō / Kyorai / Bonchō's 1690 collaborative renga beginning "Ichinaka wa..." ["Downtown..."]'. Writing separately, we agreed in advance only that each stanza should end with the word "and"; neither of us had heard the complete text until we performed it together at Openned very shortly after its composition.

DING-DONG PATTERSONG is a set of escapological variations on Don Paterson's poem 'The Wreck', which is given in full in the first section of the piece (and reprinted here without permission).

FREE ELECTRIC HERNIA, a mash-up of news reporting of the financial crisis of late 2008, an encyclopaedia article on abdominal hernia, and the lyrics of 'Free Electric Band' by Albert Hammond, topped off with a distended Rorschach inkblot, was created for a gig at the Klinker at a time when legendary impresario Hugh Metcalfe was thus incapacitated.

BLURT STUDIES: two from a set of seven heavily graphic panels for vocal performance, collaging a variety of images and variously (il)legible texts, with an emphasis on the medical, the esoteric and the pornographic.

O VIENNA is a score for performance—designed, in other words, to be interpreted (by a dancer, say) rather than read. Originally intended to be a much larger work, framed by a submerged and convoluted narrative involving figures such as Paul Celan and the *Aktionismus* artist Rudolf Schwarzkogler, but abandoned when the structural design and extensive research notes were lost in a hard drive crash. The piece as published here first appeared in Alison Croggon's excellent online journal *Masthead*.